Yesteryear I Lived in Paradise

The Story of Caladesi Island

Myrtle Scharrer Betz outside her home on Sutherland Bayou, Palm Harbor, Florida, where she wrote *Yesteryear I Lived in Paradise*. (Courtesy of the *St. Petersburg Times*.)

Yesteryear
I Lived in Paradise

The Story of Caladesi Island

BY

Myrtle Scharrer Betz

NEW AND ENLARGED EDITION

University of Tampa Press • Tampa, Florida

The University of Tampa Press
401 West Kennedy Boulevard
Tampa, FL 33606

ISBN 978-1-59732-032-0 (hbk.) • ISBN 978-1-59732-033-7 (pbk.)

**Browse & order online at
http://utpress.ut.edu**

Library of Congress Cataloging-in-Publication Data

Betz, Myrtle Scharrer, 1895-1992.
Yesteryear I lived in paradise : the story of Caladesi Island / by Myrtle Scharrer Betz. -- New & enlarged ed.
p. cm.
1st ed.: S.l. : s.n., c1984.
ISBN 978-1-59732-032-0 (cloth : alk. paper) -- ISBN 978-1-59732-033-7 (paper : alk. paper)
1. Betz, Myrtle Scharrer, 1895-1992. 2. Betz, Myrtle Scharrer, 1895-1992--Childhood and youth.
3. Caladesi Island (Fla.)--Social life and customs. 4. Country life--Florida--Caladesi Island--History--20th century. 5. Outdoor life--Florida--Caladesi Island--History--20th century. 6. Caladesi Island (Fla.)--Biography.
I. Title. F317.P6B48 2007
975.9'63--dc22   2007025625

Born to Seaward

Knowing how sea oats lean upon the wind,
Their silken rustle as they bend and sway,
And having had the sound of breakers dinned
Into your ears day after long bright day,
How can you turn you inward with good grace;
Toward towering mountains or a fertile land?
How can you even dare to set your face
Away from sea oats leaning to the sand?

You will not love the wheat fields or the corn,
The mighty rivers or the shallow rills;
Not in a thousand years, if you were born
To seaward, will you come to love the hills.
Better to give up all else than to be
Your whole life sick for sea oats and the sea.

Anonymous

Homestead Certificate No. 12580 for Henry Scharrer's acreage on Caladesi Island, issued at Gainesville, Florida, and signed by Grover Cleveland on January 23, 1897.

Contents

The Scharrer homestead on Caladesi Island.

AN APPRECIATION

By Christopher Still

It was my privilege to grow up in Florida—playing in woods and vacant lots, searching the beach, and throwing my net for mullet in the backwaters and creeks along the coast. Caladesi Island for me and many others has always been a place to explore, sometimes taken for granted because it is so close by, but always special. On the Island you can feel truly in the hands of nature. Stories have always circulated about the family that once lived on the Island, and how these early pioneers braved the heat, mosquitoes, and storms and met all of their needs without modern conveniences. As I heard their stories, they always made me wonder if I could survive in such a place. Would I be happier living such a hard but in some ways more simple life?

Even as a young man my passion was to create artwork that led people to see the beauty of Florida the way I experienced it as a child. I set out to Philadelphia and Europe to gain the skills I needed to return to Florida and depict its history and natural places in works of fine art. For over twenty years now I have traveled my home state searching for its most compelling stories. Having been honored to get to know some of the original author's surviving family members—daughter Marion and granddaughters Terry Fortner and Suzanne Thorp—I believe the story of the Scharrer family best captures for me what it means to really know and love Florida. It seems to me that the history and heart of Caladesi Island and the Scharrer family will always be linked. I believe that in Myrtle's life, in her writings, and in her passion for preserving the heritage of her family and the Island, she has given our state and nation a great gift. Their story is not just the story of one family, or one island; it is to me a universal story of family, a story of a father's love for his daughter, a story of tragedy and hope, and a story of Florida's history along the Gulf Coast.

As a father myself, I can only imagine how proud Henry Scharrer would be to know what Myrtle, her daughter Marion Ann, and her grandchildren have helped accomplish by keeping their family legacy and the Island's heritage alive in this beautiful book and in so many other ways. I feel a great sense of gratitude to Myrtle and her family for their continued passion for Caladesi Island and their unique role in its preservation. Perhaps the best way I can thank them is to try and follow their example, living in awe of the world around us, appreciating the good despite the bad, and preserving as much as possible of what is most important for future generations.

The protection of Honeymoon Island and Caladesi Island as State Parks has been made possible by the hard work of many dedicated, and hard-working members of the community, as well as the staff of the Florida State Park System. Its future depends on all of us.

February 5, 2007

FOREWORD TO THE FIRST EDITION

Those of us who have spent time in this beautiful little corner of the world cherish happy memories of sunlit days and moonlit nights boating and picnicking in and around Caladesi Island. The island has a special place in our hearts, and so does the little baby girl who was born there February 22, 1895. Her story is a unique part of the history of Florida, which we believe should be preserved for future generations.

Growing up on "Hog Island," as it was often called, the little girl became a kindred spirit with the trees and the birds, the sea oats and the little wild animals. But being raised by a man, she did a man's work when other children were playing. She was her father's fishing partner, knew how to use tools, handle a boat, and throw a mullet net. She was cook, gardener, farmer, commercial fisherman, fur trapper, ornithologist, botanist, wife, mother, grandmother, writer for sports and nature magazines, newspaper reporter, author of "Pinch Hitting for the Old Salt" (a weekly feature of the *Dunedin Times* in the 1940s), and, as friends describe her, "a character" and "the sweetest little lady I know."

Between Myrtle Scharrer Betz and her granddaughter, Terry Thorp Fortner, there is no generation gap but only mutual admiration and love. "Grandma's life has often been difficult," says Terry, "but I have always felt her strong joy in living and her deep appreciation of God's world."

Today, February 22, 1985, Myrtle Scharrer Betz is 90 years old. And today this booklet is lovingly dedicated to that sweet and spunky little lady by many friends and admirers who have made this publication possible.

Vivien Skinner Grant
Dunedin, Florida
February 1985

FOREWORD TO THE SECOND EDITION

My maternal grandmother, Myrtle Scharrer Betz, lived an extraordinary childhood in unique circumstances. She was born on February 22, 1895, on Caladesi Island, a strip of crystal white beach, oak hammock, and pinewoods, which lies in the Gulf of Mexico two miles off Dunedin, Florida.

In that time and place, growing up as an only child on an island, having lost her mother at the age of seven years, she developed a remarkable ability to listen, to wonder, to observe, and to remember. Her father instilled in his daughter a respect for nature and all living creatures. She was taught to protect and carefully harvest the resources of the sea and land around her. The Scharrer family sought to do as little damage to the environment as possible and to waste nothing.

The birdcalls in the woods, the tracks in the sand, the yearly cycles of wildflowers, and the ever-changing wave-washed beach were her storybooks.

She possesses a remarkable memory for the events of her childhood, many of which are described in the following pages. You may also discover more of her story "between the lines."

I believe you will come away with an appreciation of Myrtle's qualities of strength, humor, and individuality, as well as an insight into a way of life which is now gone forever.

Terry Fortner
Ozona, Florida
May 1991

FOREWORD TO THE NEW EDITION

From my point of view as a child, my grandmother Myrtle Betz was a formidable figure, larger than life, no-nonsense and capable; and I must admit to having been rather afraid of her. As I was growing up, though, she began telling stories about her life with her father on Caladesi Island, the pets she had and her experiences with nature and man. I never tired of hearing these stories and, during my visits, would often ask her to tell one or more of them again. They were better than fiction as they conjured up pictures of real life and made me wish and sometimes feel I had been there myself. I was no longer afraid of my grandmother.

During the late 1970s and early '80s I was working as a secretary to help finance my college education. My grandmother had asked me from time to time to type up some of her stories for submission to newspaper and magazine publishers, and I was privileged to be the first person to work with her manuscript for *Yesteryear*. So, the task of typing Myrtle's book has come full-circle for me, as this was my primary responsibility for this new edition.

In preparing this third edition of *Yesteryear* we began by going back to Myrtle's original hand-written manuscript. In the years since her death many more photographs and other materials, new to us, were discovered, and we have been working to catalogue and preserve them. Readers of the previous two printings will note especially the inclusion in this edition of many new photographs and a section at the end answering some questions that are often asked about other aspects of our grandmother's life and how the story went on after her father's death. Reading and re-working this manuscript has increased my love and respect for my grandmother and has been a balm to me as I hope it will be to you.

Suzanne Thorp
Cologne, Germany
February 2007

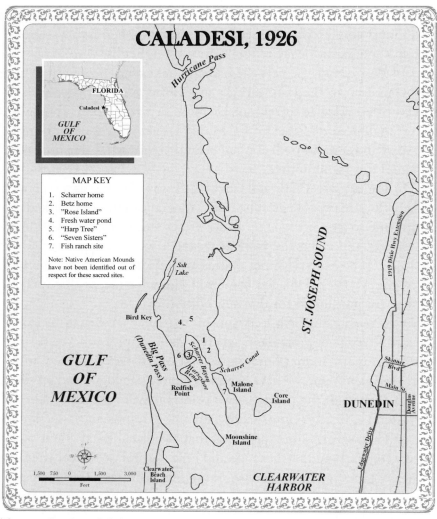

This map depicting Caladesi in 1926 shows approximate locations for sites in Myrtle's story. (Courtesy of Marcia M. Colby, Geographic Information Systems Specialist, Pinellas County Department of Environmental Management, Environmental Lands Division.)

Yesteryear I Lived in Paradise

The Story of Caladesi Island

Myrtle signing copies of the first edition of her book. (Courtesy of *St. Petersburg Times*, Sharon Kirby.)

PREFACE

This history of the Scharrer family is being put down in my 87th year. Memory is still with me. But eyesight has become so dim that I can not see what I write. So there are many mistakes in spelling. At least that is my excuse. The facts put down here are purely for the family. Over the years, much has been published in magazines and daily papers. Little has been the truth.

If Grandma Moses began painting at 70, why can't I start writing at 87?

The first part of this story is about my father before he married my mother, and I refer to him as "Henry." In the later part, which is my early life, he is "Father." The story starts with his arrival in the U.S.A. and ends with his death.

This has been written without any research, purely from memory. So this is the story of 51 years of one man's life.

Myrtle Scharrer Betz
June 10, 1981

The 23 year old man stepping ashore with pleasure. It was good to feel firm ground under his feet after a 90 day trip across the ocean. The year was April 1883. This was Henry Schairer, new from his home in Switzerland.

The crossing had been stormy with many head winds. The three masted sailing vessel was crowded, with those coming to the new land of hope. Food had to be rationed near the end of the trip and the water became stale. Suffering was great, among the women and children, and some did not make it, and were buried at sea.

Henry's parents had both died while he was yet a lad of 12. An older brother was his guardian. Full of life and the desire for adventure young Henry was signed on as cabin boy on a ship in the Mediterrean. No doubt big brother thought this would take some of the spirit out of Henry. But he loved the life on shipboard, and had won all the officers over so his lot had been easy. But off to school again. This school included the University of Zurich, where he studied to become

The first page of "New World," reproduced from Myrtle's manuscript.

NEW WORLD

The 23-year-old man stepped ashore with pleasure. It was good to feel firm ground under his feet after a 90-day trip across the ocean. The time was April 1883. This was Henry Scharrer, new from his home in Switzerland.

The crossing had been stormy with many headwinds. The three-masted sailing vessel was crowded with those coming to the new land of hope. Food had to be rationed near the end of the trip and the water became stale. Suffering was great among the women and children and some did not make it and were buried at sea.

Henry's parents had both died while he was yet a lad of 12. An older brother was his guardian. Full of life and the desire for adventure, young Henry was signed on as cabin boy on a ship in the Mediter-ranean. No doubt Big Brother thought this would take some of the spirit out of Henry. But he loved the life on shipboard and had won all the officers over, so his lot had been easy. But off to school again.

His school included the University of Zurich, where he studied to become a schoolmaster. For one who loved the outdoors and spent much time climbing the Alpine peaks hunting the wild Chamois, this was a poor choice of profession, so Henry's days of teaching were few.

Many Swiss had migrated to Wisconsin, which to them was much like their homeland. Going into the dairy business there as they had in Switzerland, they were disappointed in the dairy products. They did not come up to the standard of the old country. The Scharrers had for some generations been cheese and other dairy product producers, so the mission of Henry's trip was, in part, to visit these farmers and see, if possible, what was so different in this new country. Henry could only say it was the difference in the fodder, as Wisconsin grass was not the Alpine vegetation.

One of the first acts young Henry had taken after landing in New York City was to deposit $1,500 in a city bank. This money was to ensure return passage to his Swiss home. Hardly had he left the state when news reached him that the bank had failed and his money was lost. So now the young man was on his own. He had a smattering of the English language. Many nights, with hay for a bed and a barn lantern for light, Henry went over his English-German book trying to improve his understanding.

THE WANDERER

Now the open road called Henry and he started on his trip through the States. Sometimes by train or stagecoach, often on foot or horseback, for the next five years he wandered hither and yon. Work was to be had at farms and ranches. The going rate was $20 a month and keep. Keep was often a plate passed out the back door and a bed of hay in the barn.

A husky, willing young man could get work during harvest time or roundup most anywhere he asked for it. In some of the farm homes, the hired man had a room in the house and was treated as one of the family. If there was a town not too great a distance from the farm, everyone piled in a wagon and was off to town on Saturday night. The extra eggs and pats of butter were taken along to pay for the few things the farm did not produce. Sometimes there was a little change left over and the children could have a treat of a nickel's worth of candy. This, to the little farm folks, was pure luxury. Little hands guarded the small sack of sweets until they returned home where it was shared by all.

These little excursions made a bright spot in a dull week. The farm women met to show off the new baby, speak of their gardens and flocks of chickens. The men exchanged news of their stock or field crops. Farm boys boasted to other farm boys about the new calf that was theirs to raise.

Henry met other hired help, mainly like himself, from overseas. Many times a friendship that lasted as long as they were in the same section was started. Visits on weekends helped ease the lonesome life of drudgery.

FARM LIFE

The first one up in the morning and the last one to bed at night was the farm wife, many times going about her duties with a baby in her arms and a toddler clinging to her skirts. Henry had much admiration and pity for this member of the farm family. Coffee was ready in the early morning for the men going to the barn to feed the work stock. A huge breakfast was waiting on their return from the early morning chores. It usually consisted of a platter of fried meat, a pan of browned potatoes and a stack of hot biscuits with homemade jam and jelly. Hardly was breakfast over than the milk

Sketch by Herman Betz.

had to be cared for: cream was saved for butter; much milk was used in cooking in place of water; skim milk went to the fattening hogs and hens. The home garden and chickens were part of the farm wife's care. Three large meals a day. Then there was wash day. Wash, as a rule, was done in a cut-down wooden half-barrel. Water was pumped by hand and the pump was always near the barn, so water had to be carried for any home use. If there was an older child in the family, it was generally the duty of this child to keep the water bucket in the kitchen full.

The farm wife was nurse to anyone sick in the family and was called on to treat sick or injured farm animals. There was often no doctor available. Many times the farm mother and older children did field work if help was scarce or time was short to get in a harvest.

All the time Henry was traveling from state to state working on farms and ranches, he was writing home of his travels: the people, climate and the farming methods in the new land. These writings were being published as a feature in the local Swiss newspaper.

A winter spent in North Dakota on a cattle ranch was a lesson in how cold it could be in the States, as it went down to 60 degrees minus during the winter. Here on this ranch Henry learned there was little glamour in being a cowboy. He soon found that the dashing figure pictured was, in truth, a ranch hand and spent far more time cutting and hauling fence posts, digging post-holes and stringing barbed wire than in the saddle. Also, there were loading chutes and holding pens to repair.

Here on a cattle ranch the living was much different than on the grain farms. The help slept in bunk houses. Getting ready for a night's rest consisted of hanging your hat up and taking off your boots. A lusty call from the cook in the early morning meant "rise and shine." Meals were served in the cookhouse by a no-nonsense cook. After eating, each man washed his own plate and coffee mug and was off to whatever duty the foreman had ordered.

Sketch by Herman Betz.

DISASTER

It was at Springfield, Missouri, that Henry had an incident that may have changed his road in life. He had found "room and board" with a wheat farmer. Henry's duty was to milk and care for a small herd of dairy cows. The talk was about nothing but the great future of wheat. There being a quarter section of good land joining the farm he was working on, he wrote to his brother a most glowing letter. If they could buy this 160 acres, it would be a fine investment in this land of America. So the money was sent and Henry became a land-owner. Buying a good team of sturdy horses, Henry started breaking the land for planting. Every spare minute from farm chores Henry spent with team and plow, only stopping to water and grain-feed his team at noon. Then he would go to the farm house for a bite of food and back to the field.

One hot day, Henry did not come to the house at noon. His team was seen standing in one place, so some of the farm family went to see what was wrong. Henry was lying on the ground unconscious. A doctor was called and he said Henry had suffered a severe sunstroke. After many weeks of care, Henry regained his strength but decided he had had enough of farming. For much less than he paid for it, he gave the land to the good people who had taken care of him and was off again to another state.

PRAIRIE FIRES

In Kansas, Henry saw the dreaded prairie fires, the horizon aglow with distant fires sweeping through the grasslands. These fires took everything in their path, often farm homes and crops. They traveled faster than a man could run. The smoke and heat were intense. The only weapon against them was backfire. Farmers plowed fire lanes outside of their property then burned wide areas outside the plowed lanes. Everyone turned out to help. A shift in the wind would often be the only chance for safety. Neighbors helped neighbors. Often the farm home and buildings were saved but the fields were blackened, a year's labor lost. These fires were a yearly threat; no doubt most of them were started by dry lightning.

At one time, the Indians had been blamed as the cause of the prairie fires. When a fire had passed with no loss it was a time to celebrate, and that meant a gathering around a table loaded with food and a prayer of thanks. As time went on, the prairie fires were controlled by the land being all under plow, but then dust storms took place in drought years and erosion in times of heavy rains.

CAMP MEETINGS

It was not all work on the far-flung farms and ranches, for in the fall, when crops were laid by, there came the looked-for camp meetings. The spot picked was as central as possible and always there had to be water and grazing. People came in covered wagons, on horseback and afoot. Tents and shelters were put up; a cook site was chosen. Each

Dressed up and loaded in the wagon for a visiting day.

family brought whatever they had the most of. Several arrived with the family milk-cow tied to the back of a wagon. Some ranchers would bring a yearling steer to be butchered and cooked over hardwood coals. Everyone had a duty. The men gathered and chopped the wood for the cook fires and for the night bonfires. The bigger boys kept the water pails full. The women and older girls cooked and set tables. Old folks kept their eyes on the little children and toddlers. This was a time to renew friendships from other years and make new ones. In the evenings, there was Bible reading and singing and later, music and dancing. The circuit rider came by, giving one of his sermons warning people against sin. The service was always the highlight of the camp time. Some farmers and ranchers could stay but a few days; others, with help left at home, spent two weeks. When at last it was time to break camp, many tearful goodbyes were said and they promised that they would all meet again another year.

A HORSE NAMED PET

Each move carried our young Swiss Henry westward. He was now traveling by horseback. In the St. Louis stockyards he had bought a young dapple-grey mare, a pretty, strong animal with black mane and tail and four black feet. Her name was Pet, and pet and companion she became to a lone young man in a wild, strange land. This turned out to be a horse among horses. She never needed to be tied or hobbled at overnight camps; Henry would unsaddle Pet and she would seek grazing. He always saw to it that his horse had had water or that it was available near the overnight camp; in the early morning a sharp whistle would bring Pet on the gallop. Many mornings Henry awoke early to see Pet either standing near his tent or shelter or, if there was a clear sandy place, she, too, might be lying down. When she saw her master out, she would roll, then get up and come to him with a whinny. Henry's breakfast was usually a flapjack and Pet shared a taste. In the saddle bag there was a handful of oats or other grain for this most unusual horse. Then they were off for another day's travel. What would the day hold? Rain, hail, snow, dust storms, heat and cold. This trip across the states was not a journey of weeks or months, but of several years, so all sorts of conditions were encountered. Often the months of the most trying weather were spent on a farm working to board a man and his horse. Always there were streams and rivers to cross, mountains to climb. Now Pet had thrown a shoe and would become lame if traveled too far. So Henry was glad to come upon a farmstead. He received a warm welcome when he asked for a night's lodging and a chance to shoe his horse. The family consisted of Father, Mother and four girls. The father, recovering from an injury, would be very glad to have help. As it turned out, Henry spent the winter months with this family, only taking again to the trail after the rush of spring work was past. This proved one of the most pleasant of Henry's many "hired-man" experiences. The family took him in as one of them. He had a room in the house. Pet had a small pasture and a stall in foul weather. There were four girls, no boys, in the family. All had to pitch in to help with the farm work while their father was laid up. The apple of her father's eye was Tessie, the youngest, still in school, with a pigtail down her back; she made up for the son the father didn't have. It was Tessie that came in from the fields with a brace of rabbits for the table, Tessie who returned from the creek with a pan of fish for supper and Tessie who tamed and trained the new colt.

THE NIGHT OF THE COYOTES

For a long time Tessie had made mention of a ride she wished to take to a distant landmark called Faraway Peak. One Sunday after church, Tessie decided she was going to ride there. Henry was elected to go with her. So, saddle bags filled with lunch and canteens of water, the two young folks started off. At late noon, when they stopped for lunch, the peak seemed no nearer, and as they advanced it seemed to retreat. As the sun got low in the west, Henry said they should return home and leave the trip for another day when they could make an earlier start, but Tessie begged to go just a bit more. As the sun got low, Henry insisted they head for home. Dusk came on fast. The horses, tired from being pushed, started to stumble and falter. Henry realized that sooner or later one would go down with a possible broken leg. Seeing in the failing light a small stand of trees that would give some shelter from the chilly wind that had sprung up, they headed the horses for it. Nothing to do but spend the night. The horses were unsaddled and tied. Tessie did not seem disturbed, saying she had spent many nights camping out in the open. Henry gathered fallen limbs and soon had a cheerful fire going. They shared the remains of their ample lunch. Henry shared the remains of his canteen of water with the horses, pouring it in the crown of his hat where each horse got a few swallows. Tessie, with her saddle as a pillow and saddle blanket for a cover soon was, to all appearances, sound asleep and unworried. Soon after dark, coyotes started yipping and howling in the distance; as the night wore on they seemed to surround the campsite. The horses were nervous, pulling on their tie ropes and snorting. Petting and talking to quiet them, Henry kept up the fire. A horned owl on silent wings lit in an overhead tree and started its eerie call of five "who-who's." It was answered in the distance by another of its kind. Once there was silence followed by a blood-curdling scream: maybe only a rabbit caught by a coyote. Henry had camped in many states and heard all of this many times before, but on this night it seemed much more vivid to him. Dawn finally came, a streak of light in the east, and the end of the night's chorus. Henry called to Tessie to wake up and ride. The horses were rested and knew there was grain and water waiting for them at the farm, so by sunrise the young people were in the farmyard where a search party was forming. To the relief of all, it was seen it was not needed, and a happy group filed into the farm kitchen for a belated breakfast.

WESTWARD AGAIN

After the rush of spring planting, Henry prepared to leave what had been his home for nearly a year. The farmer had recovered from his injuries and could once again take over the heavy work. It was a sad parting from this good family, but it was once again the call of the open road. Pet was in good flesh and as eager as Henry to travel, always westward. With wages from the last months saved, Henry was not now looking for work, only to travel steadily and make time towards his objective, the Pacific Coast. It was in Indian Territory (Oklahoma) that Henry came on a company of soldiers. The officer in charge questioned him closely about who he was, where he had been and where he was going. Then the officer told him there were outlaw Indians about; farms had been burned and people murdered. Henry was informed that he was in grave danger traveling alone. Just short of an order, the officer said for his safety he must stay with them. Ever since leaving the cities, Henry had been seeing Indians, had worked with them on ranches, spent many nights sleeping in the shelter of Indian camps, had shared meals at their cook fires. So far he had found them friendly and kindly. But this might be different. Also, in the back of his mind was the idea that his horse might get some grain and he himself some well-cooked food. Several days after this, the company came on a small encampment of Indians. There seemed to be only women, children and a few old men. At once the soldiers started to be very harsh and gruff, yelling and cursing and slapping the children. Henry could see no call for their action and wanted no part in it, so he mounted his horse and rode off without as much as a goodbye.

Now as Henry moved westward, the great bands of pigeons that had filled the air, the startled deer that had bounded off, were replaced by pronghorns on the flatland. Heat waves shimmered in the distance and dust devils chased each other from west to east. This was a land of little water. On finding a small stream shaded by a cottonwood, Henry camped for a day to rest both man and horse. There was a chance to wash dust and sweat out of much-worn clothes and to bathe. Pet, too, waded in and splashed cool water over her grey, dust-covered coat. But such stops were few. Many nights' camps were dry camps and sometimes hungry camps. The cottontail rabbits that had often provided a meal were replaced by long-eared jackrabbits that were tough and strong-flavored and only eaten as a last resort. Here and there Henry came on small adobe one-room homes in a yard of greenery. The smiling brown-skinned owners, in return for a piece of silver, would share a meal of beans and corn and there would be a nubbin or two of corn for Pet. Everywhere Henry stopped, he found the people poor but friendly. Those who could speak English were hungry for news of the outside world. Some time later, Henry came on a cow camp. Cattle were being brought in from all the surrounding ranches and would later be driven to Kansas City. He enjoyed a few days' rest, a chance to mix and talk, besides some good food cooked by the usual "no foolishness" cook.

So at last, the long trip across the States was nearly over. San Francisco was only a matter of days away. On Henry's arrival in this busy, bustling city that had everything, he found a livery stable that would board his horse and allow him a bunk to sleep in. In return he was to feed and groom the stable's horses. One of Henry's first acts was to seek a barber shop, then to discard trail clothes for city raiment. Boots were displaced by shoes and a store-bought suit took the place of the jacket, shirt, trousers and chaps. Looking at himself in a mirror, Henry didn't know if he liked the new man as well as the lone traveler that had covered so many miles. But now to see the city: first the docks, lined with tall masts; here were ships with home ports on the Atlantic. They had made the rough trip around the Horn, and out of their holds came the much-needed supplies of this growing city. Then, on to see the Pacific Ocean. Henry walked the beach, smelling the tang of the sea, and was reminded of his plan to go to a southern port on the Gulf of Mexico, outfit a small boat and sail among the islands to South America before returning to his Swiss home. This was not to be, but at the time he did not realize it.

A HARD PARTING

Now Henry had a worry, and the answer was hard to find: what to do with Pet? The livery stable had offered to buy her, but she should have a better home than that. Henry thought back to the several years she had been his one friend and companion, through the snow of mountain passes, lashing rain, the heat of the desert and dry camps where she had neither water nor food. All those miles Pet had carried him, obeying every command, sometimes trembling with tiredness, but always willing to go on. What reward could one give such a faithful friend? Then, while exercising Pet in Golden Gate Park, Henry had dismounted in the shade of a tree and a young girl came up to him. She asked if his horse was for sale; all the time talking to him she was petting the horse. She explained that her father would buy her a saddle horse as soon as she found one she liked. She told Henry this was just the kind of horse she had dreamed of. The girl explained that her father was across the street waiting for her in his buggy with the bay horse. So Henry, on the spur of the moment, thought this might be the answer. He told the young lady he would sell his horse. So, after speaking to the father, he was given their address and asked to call at the house later in the day. With heavy heart, Henry looked up the address given him and found a very fine large home with surrounding grounds. On going to the door he was met by a servant who asked him in and said he was expected. Soon, the gentleman and his daughter appeared. The girl asked if she might ride the horse while Henry and her father talked. The girl was in riding habit and Henry saw by the way she mounted and took the reins, that she was used to riding, and Pet moved off with her smartly. Henry was invited into a study, offered a drink, which he refused, but did say he would like coffee, which the manservant brought. The question of price came up and, much to the surprise of the gentleman, Henry said he wanted no money, only a promise that his horse was to have a good home with proper care. Henry explained to the gentleman something of what the horse had meant to him. On being offered a token payment, he refused, saying he could not sell a loyal friend. At this time the young lady came dashing in all aglow and said that the horse was wonderful. Henry signed a sales slip and was ready to leave when the father asked him if he wouldn't be their guest for a few days. He refused with thanks, saying he was arranging to leave Frisco as soon as he could get transportation. After hearty handshakes and promises, as Henry was going out the door, the young lady threw her arms around him and kissed him on the cheek. Henry hurried down the street; he did not want anyone to see his moist eyes.

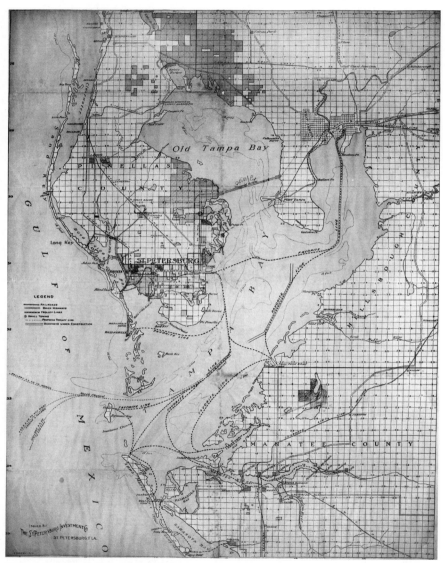

This map of the St. Petersburg-Tampa area, circa 1912, published originally in a large, color format by the St. Petersburg Investment Company, shows the port and rail connections as well as the difficulty of travel from the Island to Tampa by boat. (Special Collections Department, University of South Florida, Tampa Library.)

THE DAYS AHEAD

Henry went to a theater, had a meal in a good restaurant, then went to his lodgings to write home and give a forwarding address of Tampa, Florida. It would be six months before he would have return mail. Now to pack; the saddlebags and bed-roll were discarded. His few possessions went into a suitcase. The one concession was his rifle that had been with him in all his travels and had provided many a meal of game to be cooked over a late night cook fire (Henry had spent three years in the Swiss army serving his country and was an expert sharpshooter). Always called "the Marlin," it was broken down, carefully wrapped and strapped to his suitcase. Making his way afoot, Henry headed for the railroad station and found there would be a train out that night for New Orleans. He bought a ticket and sat waiting for its departure.

On arrival in New Orleans, Henry went to the docks, found a ship sailing for Tampa, and embarked, wondering what was ahead of him. He had a plan. Tampa, a port, would have work; he would seek a job and look for the kind of small boat he required for his exploration trip.

Again in the port of Tampa, tall-masted ships were loading and unloading cargo. Great stacks of lumber were piled on decks headed for Cuba. Henry heard much Spanish spoken. First, he needed to find a place to board. On a side street a neat frame house had a "room for rent" sign. An elderly couple showed Henry a sparsely-furnished but clean room and the young man was at home again. He learned the name of his hosts was Fribley. They were living on a forty-acre orange grove that they had lost in a freeze some years before. Their only child, a young man of 20, had sailed out of Tampa and was never to be heard of again. Henry was to hear this story often, and the old folks hoped that some day there would be a tap on the door and their son would stand there in the uniform of a sea captain.

A trip to the post office brought a surprise: letters from home and a fat money draft. This was to be used for fare home if the young wanderer was tired of roaming. But the dream of a cruise to South America was still strong. So now Henry started looking for work. A hotel was being built on the west bank of the Hillsborough River. The river ran through the town. On asking the foreman on the hotel site for a job, Henry was told that men were needed and he could start work at once.

One day while he was on this job, a very well-dressed, dignified man came where Henry was cutting rafters and started asking questions.

The Tampa Bay Hotel under construction, circa 1890. The hotel was built across from downtown Tampa on the Hillsborough River by Henry Plant, the railroad magnate.

Henry, becoming worried about being held up on his work, said he must get busy. The man told him there was no rush, that he was the owner, Henry Plant. This hotel was the Tampa Bay Hotel. It is still a landmark in Tampa, only now it is a college.

A DESIRE FULFILLED

Walking the river edge one Sunday, Henry saw a small sloop shored up in a private yard; a weather-dulled sign on it said "For Sale." A kindly-looking lady answered Henry's knock on the door and, to his question, said the boat was for sale as it had been her husband's and she was now a widow. When he asked the price, the lady said that she only wanted to get it out of the yard and would take whatever was offered her. So here was Henry's boat!

On the following Sunday, with the help of a friend and much pushing and rolling, the boat was slipped into the river where it promptly sank—no surprise, as the seams were open from long drying out of the water. The following weekend, the boat was pumped out and rode high out of the water, some 30-feet long with smart lines. Henry was pleased with his well-built little craft, carrying the name *Anna. Anna* it would remain.

Some few weeks before the purchase of the little ship, Henry had bought a tax deed on two-and-a-half acres of land east of Sulphur Springs on the river front, facing what was known as Hanna's Whirlpool. It was here that *Anna* was to be shored up and worked on. With the last pay envelope from the hotel job, the room rent was paid and goodbye said to the old folks, then to a ship chandler's to buy white lead [i.e. lead carbonate, which was used in paint], caulking and the tools to apply it. Later, Henry looked up a sail maker and had a mainsail and jib made for the little craft. The *Anna* had a small trunk cabin. Henry added a bunk on one side of the centerboard and galley and storage space on the other. Being enough of a seaman to know that a shallow centerboard craft would not be as seaworthy as a keel (deep) craft, Henry's plans and hopes were that he might stay close to shore and search out the lee sides of islands.

SHAKE-DOWN CRUISE

At last there came a day when the last coat of paint went on, a coat of copper paint was applied, then back on the water went *Anna*. Now it was time to try out the little ship. So a shake-down cruise was planned. With food aboard for a week, down the river went *Anna* heading out of Tampa Bay in a stiff southwest wind. The small sloop sailed close to the wind, much in its favor, so little tacking was needed to reach Egmont Light[house] and the open Gulf. Heading north with a quartering wind, the sloop fairly flew along. The lone seaman was well-pleased with the performance of his ship. The seas were heavy. They could be seen breaking on the beaches. *Anna* sailed along with her lee deck under. As evening approached, angry, dark clouds gathered in the northwest and the wind became gusty. So, to look at the chart and seek shelter. A red nun buoy was close; the chart was marked Big Pass. Heading for the pass and getting in calmer water, he found a small cove or bayou. To sail into this snug harbor was next. Soon the little bayou narrowed and here anchor was dropped in shallow water, out of the seas and much of the wind force.

THE DISCOVERY

Hardly were the sails down and secured when the wind shifted with a bang and a dash of heavy rain followed. Snug in the cabin, Henry made a supper of hot coffee, bread, cheese and a sweet. The light had faded and it seemed a night for sound sleep. But first, to light the lantern, look at the chart and find what landfall this little harbor was. Marked "Hog Island," it proved to be about six miles long and about a mile-and-a-half, at the nearest point, from the mainland coast.

On awakening in the early morning, it was apparent to Henry, from the list to the cabin, that the little ship was hard aground. After a meager breakfast, he decided to wade ashore and, while waiting for the tide, to explore. The wind was out of the east; the morning sunny and brisk. The first thing Henry noticed was a great swarm of birds. There seemed to be every kind, size, and color. They were on the ground, in the trees and the air. It was the most beautiful sight he had ever seen. What he didn't know was that this was the height of the spring migration and the birds, like himself, had sought the shelter of the land during the blow. As he walked around, there were lovely, daisy-like flowers, black centers with yellow petals, covering the ground. Several huge oaks with glossy green leaves spread their limbs over a hundred feet. Every plant and tree looked fresh and green. A deer bounded away and a brown turtle hurried across an opening to disappear in a burrow. This, to the young man, looked like paradise. As he was wading out to the *Anna,* he saw a great school of fish making its way into the bayou with the incoming tide. The mullet were, in some cases, pushing each other out of the water in their haste. Henry stunned one with an oar and thought it the best fish he had ever eaten. There were only the ashes from an old campfire on shore to show that anyone had put foot here. Henry turned over in his mind the idea of owning such a piece of nature. He decided to return to Tampa and inquire how such land could be obtained.

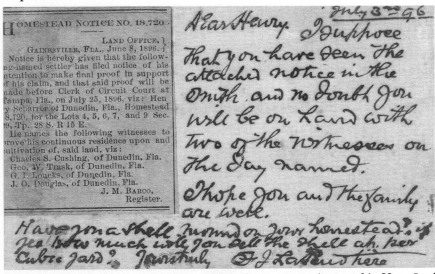

A postcard to Henry Scharrer, dated July 3, 1896, with a newspaper clipping of the Homestead Notice published by the Land Office in Gainesville, Florida, acknowledging his claim.

HOMESTEADER

A trip to a lawyer's office gave Henry the information he needed to acquire the paradise he had found. First he should become a United

States citizen, then contact the land office in Gainesville; the land could be homesteaded. The requirements were to live on the land for five years and make certain improvements: a livable house, land cleared and crops planted. After the five years were past, then with reliable witness, appear before a county judge and swear to the fact that all requirements had been met. In time came a land patent from Washington signed by Grover Cleveland. This patent was issued in 1897. It was a long time from the first time Henry saw his island until he became the owner of his 156 acres. Lots of heartbreak and hardships were in the in-between years. At first it was the matter of making the few dollars that were needed for supplies and improvements. On a trip to Dunedin, the closest town and post office, Henry met a man who offered him a job in a sawmill where, in return for labor, he would be paid in lumber to build a house. So each morning Henry rowed a small rowing scull across the sound, walked the three miles east of town to the mill and put in 10 hours of labor; then the morning trip was repeated in the evening back to the island. Came the proud day when enough wages had built up to pay for the needed lumber. So, with an ox team, it was hauled to the shore, loaded on a skiff and rowed across the sound.

Henry built a sturdy, board-and-batten, story-and-a-half home for himself. Surrounded by the limbs of the huge oak, it looked protected and blended in as part of the natural surroundings. This sturdy pioneer

The chalet-style cabin that Henry built, with sleeping loft and the added room (far right).

home stood for many years and took all the storms with only the loss of a few shingles now and again.

Another spring arrived. Again, the rush of migrant birds came as visitors for a day or week. Now there was a large garden, a flock of hens, several hives of bees and the start of a herd of pigs. There was produce to sell from door to door in town. Fish and other seafood were plentiful: oysters and stone crabs in the cool months, scallops and clams in the summer. Henry bought a gill net; the amount of fish that could be caught was only limited to what could be sold. Smoked mullet were in demand, and salt mullet in the fall.

These were the days of no refrigeration. The smoked mullet of those days was much different than the product offered today. It was dark brown in color, dry, and would keep for weeks. Tangy with salt, it was very tasty. Housewives were glad to have "the man from the island" come to their door.

Henry's bee hives. Beekeeping was a hobby and a source of income.

The stores did not carry fresh produce. The winter folks, those who came from the north and had homes (mainly along the waterfront), showed much interest, bought the produce and very often invited Henry into their homes for a chat and a cup of coffee. Always asking about his island home, these people were invited to visit it.

Many of the winter visitors owned sailboats so there were many picnic parties that visited the island. It was with pride that Henry showed these visitors over his island acres. There was a large Indian burial mound, a separate one-grave site, a sand mound, oddly-shaped trees, a fresh-water pond where the wild animals gathered to drink and, near the home site, a pair of bald eagles had built a huge nest in a tall pine tree. All of this was shown visitors on a nature walk. These visits to "Scharrer's Island" became a tradition, and over the years no winter season went by without these island visits, right up to second-generation visitors.

But there was a thorn in the flesh in this paradise. Some of the local people did not accept the foreigner. The island had been a no-man's land, where there were no rules of conduct. Fires could be set anywhere, trees cut, firewood removed and every living thing could be shot, regardless of species or season. Now, on the acres in Henry's homestead, this was something of the past. Anyone living on an island was different and therefore suspect and probably undesirable and weird. On mentioning this to the kindly postmaster and storekeeper, a Mr. Trask, the "foreigner" was assured that this would wear off in time. But it never did. It was not only the feeling of resentment that hurt; it was also much harassment and destruction of material things each time the owner was away, even to the killing and removal of livestock.

A quick trip to Tampa, then the county seat, to appear before a judge for those much-wanted citizenship papers. The judge had a stern lecture on how this country was free, not ruled as in Europe by kings

Large party of visitors on the outer beach at "Scharrer's Island."

and emperors, and how we, the people, ruled by an elected president. Henry had learned to hold his tongue and at least give the appearance always of agreeing to all said about this new country he was in. He felt much like saying that was the kind of country he had left—a free one. The little country of Switzerland had long before shed its blood for the freedom it now enjoyed. To a Swiss native there was nothing of as much importance as freedom and independence.

The trip back to the island in the little ship *Anna* was started in a heavy southwest wind. Good time was made, and on reaching the tip of Pinellas Point, instead of heading for the open Gulf, the *Anna* was headed up the sound between the islands and the mainland. Dark clouds were gathering in the northwest and there would soon be a change in wind. Also, a very high tide was rushing out at what was known as the "narrows" and is now Indian Rocks. The little craft ran aground with the heavy weather coming down and an anchor went overboard, sails were tied secure and it was a comfort to retreat to the shelter of the cabin as a dash of rain arrived with a gust of wind. The rigging slapped the mast, the turnbuckles whistled in the wind. It was a good night to have a warm meal and then settle in a bunk for a night's sleep. In the early morning, Henry woke to very chilly air out of the northeast, and from the list of the cabin he knew the little ship was fast aground. What was not visible at dusk when the anchor went out was

Henry in front of his cabin.

now much exposed mud flats and great oyster bars. On the mainland side there was a fish camp, net spreads with skiffs tied to them and among the trees, a house. Since only an incoming tide could float the *Anna,* there was little to do until the cold spell was over and high tides would return. Now seemed a good time to gather a pail of oysters, both as something in the way of food and the time passed in opening them. So with a bucket in hand, Henry waded towards an oyster bar. Hardly had he stooped to pick up the first oyster when there was a spat of mud near him and the crack of a rifle. So back to the ship, as it seemed someone on shore considered the oysters off limits for a stranded boatman. It was two nights later before there was a night tide to float the *Anna.* Henry never again used the inside route on his trips, always taking to the open Gulf.

ANOTHER NEWCOMER

Catherine McNally had come to America from Ireland with her family at the age of three. The family settled inland near Cleveland, Ohio, and carried on farming as they had in the old country. On the early death of the father and breadwinner, it became Catherine's duty as the oldest child to take over the duties of supporting the mother and young sisters and brothers. Now they were out of school and could be on their own. So, in the fall of 1893, Catherine took a position as companion to a wealthy lady from Cleveland, a Mrs. L. H. Malone. The Malone family had a winter home in Dunedin, Florida. Mrs. Malone missed the social life of Cleveland and cared little for the winter stay.

L. H. was a yachting enthusiast and spent most of his time sailing his boat, deep-sea fishing and practicing for the weekly sailing race put on by the Dunedin Yacht Club.

The three Malone children, Eleanor, Clarence and Lee, had a private tutor. There was a housekeeper and a cook. Often Mrs. Malone and Catherine would rent a rig from the local livery stable and drive the country roads. There were wild flowers to pick and pleasant lakes to sit by. The Plant hotel, the Belleview, gave musicals and put on plays and held dances, and on such occasions many of the winter visitors

The Yacht Club Inn in Dunedin, Florida, where wealthy sailing enthusiasts came to stay for the winter season. Many of the guests visited Henry at "Scharrer's Island."

sailed from Dunedin in the evenings and landed at the hotel docks to attend these affairs. So the two ladies found things of interest to do and converse about.

PIONEER COMMERCE

It should be explained here that there were general stores selling horse collars, barn lanterns, piece goods and dry groceries. As there was no refrigeration, the stores carried nothing perishable in the way of meats or vegetables. These were brought to the homes by the local farmers and fishermen who produced them. Stores were stocked with barrels of flour, sugar, rice, green coffee, dried beans, etc. The open barrels stood in a row with a scoop in them. A clerk weighed out whatever was asked for. The going price was three pounds of most anything for a quarter; very little, if any, foods came in packaging. Potatoes were sold, not by pounds but by measure—a peck, half-bushel and so on. There were great wheels of cheese with a knife by them and bacon came in slabs. These were the country stores of 1895.

To the doors of the homes came boys pulling express wagons with milk and other dairy products. Gardeners came with baskets of

The L. H. Malone home on Victoria Drive, Dunedin, where Catherine was employed.

vegetables and fishermen with dressed fish. Once a week, fresh beef arrived, drawn by a horse; the back of the buggy held cuts of beef that the housewife came out to inspect and indicate what cut she wanted. It became Catherine's duty to choose and pick from what was offered for the family menu. One of these door-to-door sellers was Catherine's favorite. That was the man from the island. With a basket on each arm he came to the door, baskets filled with garden vegetables, always so fresh and colorful, fish dressed, sometimes smoked fish. It always seemed to Catherine as if Henry's food was arranged more tastefully. So she would look across the sound and see his sailboat, looking to her like a great white bird, or sometimes on a calm day it would be the flash of oars as he crossed the stretch of water between his island home and the mainland.

MAINLAND VISITORS

Catherine often detained Henry by asking him questions about the island. Cold days he was asked in for a cup of coffee. He asked Catherine if she would care to visit his island home; she said she would like very much to do so. Mrs. Malone, who also liked to talk to Henry, said that they would arrange a picnic and arrive in Mr. Malone's sailboat. So one fair day the Malone family, with Catherine, arrived at Henry's landing. A walk was taken over the property with points of interest being shown with pride—the eagles' great nest, the burial

The Douglas-Somerville Store in Dunedin. The waterfront and pier can be seen in the background. (Courtesy of Dunedin Historical Society.)

mound of one grave, dwarf oaks surrounding it. Supposedly this was the grave of an Indian princess. Then there was the large Indian mound, the site of the village, a pine divided and grown in the shape of an Irish lyre. There was a small fresh-water pond, the watering place of the wildlife. Then, back to the house and a picnic lunch.

The children were pleased to feed a mother pig and her eight black, white-belted babies and a hen with a dozen chicks. After lunch, the children climbed the sprawly limbs of the huge oak that sheltered the house. Mr. Malone dozed in the shade of a palm tree while Henry showed the ladies the inside of his house—everything in place, clean, neat and simple; the wood stove polished, shiny black; pots and pans hanging on hooks. Sleeping quarters were in the half-story garret reached by a wide-stepped ladder. Henry was pleased to offer the ladies tea, fresh bread of his own baking and honey. The children came in for the bread and honey part. So now Catherine had seen how the lone islander lived. She loved the freedom, being removed from the cares of the world and the simplicity of living. Sometime shortly after their island visit, Henry, taking a deep breath and hoping for the right answer, asked Catherine if she would share his life and Catherine's answer was "Yes."

Catherine "Kate" McNally Scharrer. (Courtesy of the Dunedin Historical Society, Malone Album.)

[29]

A MOONLIGHT WEDDING

On a full moonlit night in April 1894, the wedding party, with a Reverend Brown to officiate, rowed across Saint Joseph Sound and Henry and Catherine became husband and wife. The group gathered in a palm grove north of the house where the vows were said. After a wedding feast held outdoors, the attendants returned across the sound and Henry and Catherine were alone in their paradise. (This is the story of Myrtle's father and mother.)

Now Catherine busied herself about making her new house a home. She had a set of dishes, silverware and linens and a rug for the floor. Soon the house showed the touch of a woman. This all was very pleasing to Henry. Maybe more than all these house improvements, Henry was pleased to find that Catherine was an outstanding cook. Her food was very tasty and attractively served. Nothing seemed to please her more than to have guests in for a meal and surprise them with a new dish. The masterpiece was a roast suckling pig, stuffed with savory spices and herbs, browned to a turn with crisp skin that on being pierced with a fork ran rich with juice, always served with honey-glazed sweet potatoes and mashed turnips. It was with a lot of pride that these home-cooked meals of products produced on the island farm were served.

Soon Catherine's cooking fame spread and many from the Yacht Club Inn were asking if they could be paying guests. In those days, there were no restaurants as such. Anyone wishing to eat out made an appointment at a hotel. A General Sherman from the yacht club was a frequent visitor, bringing a half-dozen friends with him. Catherine's table would be set with a snow-white linen tablecloth, dishes and silver polished and gleaming. There was always a flower arrangement of the native island plants and flowers or a scene in miniature. Once, there was a beach with rocks, sand and shells and a tiny toy boat; always clever and colorful.

Like all folks starting out a new life, Henry and Catherine had many plans and hopes for the future. Among them was to have a dining area to serve meals. With all the products from the land, it seemed a dream that could come true. A deepening of the small waterway into

Marriage certificate for Henry Scharrer and Kate McNally, dated April 14, 1894.

the bayou would be called for, as at low tide the larger boats could not reach the landing dock. So, many evenings were spent making future plans that might make them more comfortable in the way of extra money. Around this time, an ice plant was started in Clearwater and a fish house now could ship fish by express train to nearby states. The amount of fish that could be caught was only limited by the amount the fish house could handle. So Henry gave up his trips peddling fresh produce in town, bought more and better gear to fish with and became a commercial fisherman. He also gave over more time to his herd of hogs, as he found a ready market for freshly-dressed pork.

ANOTHER ISLANDER

Now, to their joy, they found that a child was to join them, and on February 22, 1895, a baby girl arrived. A midwife was on hand ahead of time; also, one of the worst storms of the winter season. As things didn't go as well as expected, a worried Henry rowed the sound in a gale of wind to get a doctor. The storm became so violent that it was impossible for him to return. To complicate matters, a stranded couple from Dunedin who had come to the beach for a day's outing sought refuge in the Scharrer home. It was not until the following morning that a Dr. Edgar from Clearwater was brought over, and in the afternoon the baby girl arrived to see what all the excitement was about. Catherine always told of a beautiful small blue bird that came into the house to get out of the storm and perched on the footboard of her bed. This was an indigo bunting.

Catherine, wearing the black dress she had for special occasions, and the Malones at the homestead. (Courtesy of the Dunedin Historical Society, Malone album.)

The child was born to the sound of the pounding surf on the outer beach, the whine of the wind in the eaves. Forever this child would love nature above all else; wildlife would be her friends and companions. The baby was named Myrtle, after the wax myrtle that grew on the island. Catherine had gathered its fragrant berries to make sweet-smelling candles. Henry and Catherine felt the little addition to their home was a blessing and the child grew up knowing no bitterness. Henry was making a tomboy of her by making wooden toys of guns and boats, while Catherine was trying to interest her in house work, cooking, and doing fancy work, as Catherine was fond of making lace.

The 1899 receipt for taxes paid by Henry Scharrer to Hillsborough County. Signed by tax collector M. J. McMullen.

HEARTBREAK ENTERS EDEN

There were some years of happiness and freedom for the family and then Catherine became ill. Anything local doctors could do did not seem to help. Slowly her health failed to where she took no interest in her riding horse, a gift from Henry. The long walks on the beach were no more. In the spring of 1902, Catherine was taken to a doctor's home in Clearwater to have an operation, which it was hoped would bring her back to health. So the little family boarded their sailboat, leaving their island home in the hands of no one, but with the hope they might soon return. But it was not to be.

At the doctor's home there were two boys, one Myrtle's age, one older. Never having had children to play with, it seemed to come natural to Myrtle to want to be part of the gang. She tagged the boys, much to their disgust, wherever they went (as that's where the action was), and the town's dock was visited. Small ships were coming in and unloading freight, fishermen with their catches loading the fish in horse-drawn wagons and party boats taking off with tourists for a sail about the harbor or a picnic and shelling trip to the nearby island beaches.

On this one morning, Myrtle, tagging along with Marcus and Buford, fell off the dock into twelve feet of water. The child could not swim and would have drowned but for the quick thinking of 12-year-old Buford. He jumped down into a skiff that was tied to the dock and hauled the little girl out. Wet but unhurt, all but for a badly-scraped leg, cut on barnacles. While she was catching her breath and dripping wet, the younger brother, Marcus, asked what she was going to tell about this accident and she replied, "I'm not going to tell them anything." So it seems a very brave, quick-thinking boy was cheated out of his dues as a lifesaver. The oddity of this incident is that the boy was the son of the doctor who had delivered the little girl. So two in the same family helped to give her life. The Edgar boys grew into fine young men. Both went to New York City and were successful in business.

[From now on Myrtle tells her story in the first person.—ed.]

Early one morning in April 1902, Father came into my room at the Edgars' home and said, "Mother left us last night, Myrtle. We will be going home this evening. Before she left she said to tell you 'good-bye'." So that's how I knew my mother was dead, that now it was only my father and me.

The casket stood on trestles in the Edgars' living room. It was black with a silver dove on the top. Ladies from a nearby church came in to sing my mother's favorite, "Jesus, Lover of My Soul," among other hymns; a minister said a few words. As I stood staring at the casket with a jumble of thoughts, one of the ladies asked me, "Do you know what's in there?" I said, "Yes, it is my mother." Then she said, "You know you will never see her again." I answered in some heat, "Yes, I will, in Heaven." This was my mother's teaching spoken out. So my dear, beautiful mother was laid to rest in the Clearwater cemetery. Those were the days when the mourners stayed to see the grave mounded up. I can still hear the shovels full of earth echoing as they filled the grave. My mother, with the laughing blue eyes, the lilting, soft voice, milk white skin, and red hair which when let down hung to her waist.

The only surviving photo of the entire Scharrer family. From left to right: a female friend, Catherine, Myrtle as a toddler, and Henry.

Myrtle, age 7, and her father at their island homestead. Photo by Dr. Badeau, a friend from Dunedin.

Three

A SAD HOMECOMING

It seemed wrong to me as my father and I went out to the sloop moored offshore, the one that had brought us from the island some weeks before, that Mother was not to go home with us. The Edgar boys had been persuaded by their mother to give me their small, brown dog, saying to the boys, "You have each other; Myrtle doesn't have anyone." So a heart-broken man, a small, seven-year-old girl and a little brown dog sailed in the late afternoon for their island home. It was a silent trip. Father, too full of grief to say anything, and I, not understanding what the future would hold.

On landing and approaching the house, we could see that something didn't look as it had been left. The house had been entered; everything was in a shambles as we opened the door. Everything of value had been taken. Mother's china and silver were gone. There was the wood cook stove, a few chairs, the kitchen table; that's about all that was left.

My father, speechless for a minute, looked over the scattered few things left, then turned to me and said, "We will have to start over again, Myrtle." The one great loss we felt most was my mother's trunk. In it was the one photo we had had of her. I've always felt that whoever did it (and Father had a very good idea who it was) had only taken the picture because they did not notice it. The only one remaining picture of Mother is a snapshot of her, a friend, me at two years of age, and my father standing some distance away [see page 35].

In the shambles on the floor was a broom. I picked this up and started to sweep the litter together. It was late evening; Father started

Myrtle and Henry under one of the oak trees that sheltered their home.

a fire in the wood cook stove and made us a supper of groceries he had brought from town. Neither of us was the least bit interested in food. Right then I was cheered by the old cat that we had left coming to the door. Flossie had been my companion as long as I could remember. Somehow she had fed herself over the weeks we were gone. She seemed happy to see us and was given a saucer of canned milk, which she finished with gusto. Oddly enough, the garret, which had been my bedroom, had not been disturbed. It contained little but a double bed, table, chair, lamp and clothes chest. So, as dark came on, I went up the ladder and took comfort in a familiar place.

This garret room was mine for the twenty years I lived with my father. I always felt secure in it. On stormy nights gusts of wind would sometimes make the house tremble; rain on the wooden shingles lulled me to sleep. During heavy weather I could hear the pounding of the surf on the outer beach. On calm nights the voices of the sea-birds came to me as they gathered on a barrier sand reef off the beach. There was the sweet whistle of the black-bellied plover; sometimes a Ward's heron (now called "great blue") flew over the roof giving a harsh call that for a moment startled me. In the early mornings I often awoke to the song of a mockingbird perched on the roof tree.

BLOOD RELATIONS

Father wrote to Mother's family telling them of her death. A sister of Mother's named Martha wrote back saying she would take Catherine's child if my father was unable to care for it. Father read me part of the letter he wrote back, in which he said, "I'm not willing to give up my little daughter." In no way could I have ever repaid my father for his care, teachings and sacrifices made through the years. I was not as thoughtful a daughter as I might have been, and I owe my father many thanks he never got. There is no turning back to go over things a second time, but in my heart I will always regret the many chances missed to make life a little happier for a very kind, thoughtful man.

Little thanks or appreciation did Mother get for her years of providing for her family of brothers and sisters. In all the years, I never received any greeting or little gift from them, and none of Mother's personal possessions ever came my way, among them $1,500 in savings she had left with them. Father sent the family gifts several times. Once it was a brass-bound cypress bucket full of choice shells Mother had cleaned and polished, thinking they would like something their sister had handled and valued. I'm sure they thought it was best not to have memories of their dead sister.

CHILDHOOD ENDS

Father, a few days after our return home, went looking for his herd of hogs and found over half of them had been stolen during our weeks of absence. The island was nearly six miles long. There were no fence laws, so stock was allowed to roam, and hogs will travel great distances hunting for food.

Pine saplings had been cut and several enclosures made over the property where the hogs had been either baited with corn or driven in by dogs. Father's pigs, black with white bands over their shoulders, showed up all over the county, where before the natives had kept what was called razorback hogs, any color and tall and thin in build. This hog stealing had been going on for many years but not in such a grand style.

This was a hard blow, as there were doctor bills, board bills, and funeral expenses that Father had meant to meet with the sale of dressed pork. This, young as I was, distressed me, as I could see how worried and concerned my father was. Somewhere along here my childhood ended. Now I had duties I was expected to perform. There was a wood-box to keep full and water to carry in; there must always be a pailful in the house. The floor must be swept, the dishes washed, the chickens were to be fed in the morning and evening and their door must be closed after they went to roost at night or coons would make off with the laying hens. If there were pigs penned and fattening, they must be fed and watered. To me it seemed endless, but I took pleasure in being "so big" that I could help.

About this time, Father started getting me to help prepare our simple meals. This suited me fine; it was like playing house in a real way. Before I knew it, I was making all the meals, and now I was taught how to make bread. This I really liked. There was so much satisfaction in seeing the fragrant brown loaves come out of the oven; and oh how wonderful to have the privilege of cutting off the warm heel and eating it. No cake ever tasted so good. So with me learning to take over the house duties, my father was once again free to fish, see to the few remaining hogs and plant a large patch of sweet potatoes that could be sold for a dollar a bushel.

Myrtle posed to show off her long hair.

GIFTS FROM THE SEA

But it was not all work, it seemed every week there was something of interest to do or see. If there had been a winter blow, the beach would be newly covered with colorful shells of all kinds. Sometimes there was a real treasure to be found. Every so often there was a rare junonia, for which, if in good shape, a shell dealer would pay ten dollars. Once, in a little pearl oyster, there was a perfect pearl, small but lovely. Sometimes timber washed in—things that could be used for dock repairs and other uses. Then there were things of no value, but they held a story.

What happened to bring in the broken oar from a ship's long-boat, the name of the ship on the blade? Combing the beach to me was like turning the pages of a book. Everything held a story. The beach also was a source of food. During the month of February, a sea mustard grew above the tide mark. It was unmatched by any of the garden greens. In the summer months a little surf clam called coquina was plentiful. This made a broth much like oysters but far more delicate and delicious. So the beach had much to offer.

The wooded part of the island also had much to offer. There was always something new. Under an oak thicket were fresh cast skulls, bones and fur. So a barn owl had joined the other residents of the woods. Something new in plant life may have appeared; from where and how was always a question. In among some scrub a sand pine reared its head, something that had not been there before. On a ridge a turkey oak showed its cut leaves, a new flower bloomed; always a surprise seemed to appear. Sometimes it was a first, as when the burrowing owls came to the beach, using the ghost crab holes which the owls enlarged into their burrow. Such friendly little birds; always the pair together. In their burrows were their three or four young. The nesting material would lead one to believe that they were making a hot bed for their young: dried dung, cigarette packages, pieces of rags and on this nesting material was placed food for the little owlets. Most times it was a rat with the head eaten off. These friendly little birds, shortly after coming to the beach, met a most unjustified end. Deep-sea fishermen dragging the beach for bait saw the owls and either shot or killed them by striking them with a stick, killing them for fish bait. This was a hard blow to one who had studied them and enjoyed these very valuable birds. But there were many heartaches of this type to be endured over the years.

To the child that I was, there were new things, pleasure in every month of the year, always something to look forward to. There were the sea-foods that came seasonally, such as the stone crabs that moved on the grass flats as soon as the first cool spell of Fall came. These large crabs dug a burrow and were gathered by the use of a hook on a short pole. When the hook was put in the crabs' burrow, they would snatch the hook in their claws and allow themselves to be drawn out. We had an oyster bar, tended to keep the whelks off of it, as they, too, like oysters. Since we always returned the opened shells to the bar for the spat [an oyster spawn] to attach themselves to, this small tended bar kept us in oysters all during the cool months. In July, scallops were to be had in abundance. Earlier they were too small to gather. These lasted into late August. Always there were clams to be found on most of the grass flats. At low tide it was only a matter of walking over the flats and looking for what was called the keyhole. This was the mouth of the clam at ground level. Fish of some kind could be caught any day in the year.

Photo of Scharrer's Bayou, looking west, taken from the lookout ladder. The "Seven Sisters" are in the distance, right of center, and tiny "Rose Island" is on the left.

The fall months brought the fat mullet, later to have the delicious roe. Food for the table was always there, only needing to be gathered and prepared. As I used these foods, I thought of primitive man who had lived here, and I felt I was following his footsteps. I often wondered if small Indian children had not done just as I was doing in the same way and over the same ground.

The high land also held a food supply. The cabbage or sabal palms had a heart, the bud that could be cooked as a vegetable or used as a salad. Then there were sea grapes and fox grapes to make jelly and jam.

Henry combing Myrtle's hair. Photo by Dr. Badeau.

SCHOOL DAYS

So in these early years, while other children were learning their ABCs at a school desk, I was learning the ways of the wild. This was not always to be, as Father, in the evenings, was teaching me to read. He, himself a great reader, said once I learned to read the knowledge of the world would be at my fingertips. But there came a day when I, too, was to go to school. I was going on nine that fall and fully able to row to the mainland. My little skiff was tied up to the L. H. Malones' private dock; the oars were left on the porch in case the boat sank; and they might be ſtolen if left in the skiff.

The Malone dock, where Myrtle tied up her boat in the morning before walking to school.

The school house, a one-room frame building, was what was then known as "eaſt of town." Miss Cobb, an old maid, ſtern but under-ſtanding, was the teacher for the eight grades. Little tots barely over five to eighteen-year-olds were the pupils. There were thirty children and some families had four or five children enrolled. I will not say it was not a traumatic experience for me. I had never played with and seldom seen children. Was I scared? No, it was rather that here again was something new for me to learn about. On my firſt day, with a lunch of crackers and cheese in a bag, I arrived at the fenced-in yard, walked through the gate, hardly knowing what to do and wishing that I was on my way home across the sound. There I ſtood dumbly when a girl

Myrtle's fourth grade report card.

came down off the entrance porch, took my hand, told me her name, Bernice Andrews, and explained that the door would soon open and we could go in. Bernice, I know you are long gone from this world, but God bless you for your kindness.

Bernice was a possible two years older than I. She came from a family of seven, some older and some younger than herself. Poor Miss Cobb hardly knew where to put me. Questions: What is your name? Can you write or spell it? "Yes." Have you ever gone to school before? "No." Can you read? "Yes." Here was I, who should be in the fourth grade, started with little tots that first day. Well, that didn't last long. Seems next day I was in second grade and finally ended in the fourth grade. It was not easy to catch up with things I had missed but somehow I did it, only having a bad hangup on arithmetic.

I must explain in passing why there were older children of high school age. (We never heard of high school.) Many came from other states and had had to work on the farm. Girls had been kept out of school to help in the house and some had not lived where a school was available. No doubt the children could not help but think me strange; living on an island was not done. Islands were only to have picnics on, maybe swim and gather shells, and this on an average of once a year. Many of the children had never visited any of the offshore islands. I was even asked if I lived in a house and what we had to eat.

Myrtle with Clara Thompson, one of her schoolteachers, in the shade of trees on an Indian mound on Caladesi Island.

But my first year at school was short-lived, as my father wished to make a trip to Tampa to sell produce in the late Fall. We loaded our thirty-five foot sloop with casks of salt mullet, bushels of sweet potatoes and honey—this in friction-top cans from the American Can Company—in quarts, half-gallons and gallons. I was so proud to have labeled the honey cans with a colorful label showing a straw beehive on one side, a bunch of red clover blossoms on the other and Father's name and address at the bottom. The top of the label had the word "Honey." So early one morning we were off for the seventy-mile water trip to the "big city." With fair wind, we arrived the afternoon of the second day. Some of the produce was sold right at the dock where we moored. Wagons came down and loaded the sweet potatoes and salt fish. Then Father visited some stores with samples of the honey and soon it was all disposed of. On this trip I saw my first car, a chain drive; it crossed Platt Street Bridge at about fifteen miles an hour. Horses shied away and drivers of teams shouted at the driver in rather harsh tones. Before we were ready to sail for home, Father took me for a walk about the city. There were such wonders as I had never seen in the small towns near us; mannequins all dressed up so fine in the store windows, a Chinaman with his pigtails. I took it all in, the strange smells and sights. The Tampa Bay Hotel was, in my eyes, so huge and beautiful and it made me feel important when Father told me he had worked on it and helped build it.

PRACTICAL LESSONS

Father was teaching me to help handle the boat and a part of my duties was to haul up the mainsail, no small task for a child. First the throat halyards had to be hauled on until the gaff end was as high as it would go. That line was belayed [fastened to a cleat] and the throat halyards took the gaff up. Then the after leach [device which pulls the boom up and gives fullness to the sail] was used to trim up the sail. Now the jib was hoisted, the dock lines untied with manful shoves and pushes, the boat left the dock, the sails filled and we were on our way home.

Part of the time I was at the wheel, steering. This was the part I liked, but there were many things to learn and watch besides just keeping the sails full of wind, like which side to pass that oncoming three-masted schooner tacking in against a head wind. Father and I made many of these trips in the next few years and he seemed to trust my judgment in handling the small ship, even to night sailing in the open Gulf. There were many rules of the road to learn; also much about weather and how to detect shoal water.

Gaff-rigged "cat" boat under sail to Caladesi. (Photo repaired by Barb Carrier.)

Once, sailing in Tampa Bay, while Father was in the cabin, I saw off to the east a mist and what looked like a line of foam advancing from the distance. I called Father; he took one look and ordered, "Sails down and anchor out." I didn't know the reason for these orders but helped carry them out, and none too soon, as a gale of wind hit us and a huge wave of water came over the decks. It was all over in a few minutes. Father said this was a white squall. In later years I was to see two others.

It was always an awaited pleasure to come back home after these trips and see how the stock had fared. The hogs were well able to take care of themselves, as they could roam the thousand acres and find much food. Sometimes the chickens had suffered a raid by raccoons. Faithful old Flossie (the cat) was usually waiting on the dock for us and had a few loud protests over not having had her usual bowl of milk.

MONEY VALUES

It must have been about this time in my life that I heard children at school speak of an allowance. This was a new word to me, but I soon learned it was spending money that a child was given by its parents and could be used to buy candy or crackers. So I got up my courage (I never asked for things) and asked my father if I could have an allowance. He stopped what he was doing and looked at me a long time. I was almost scared; had I done something so wrong? Then Father said, "I will show you how to earn your allowance." This was fine with me. Some time later he gave me half-a-dozen steel traps and showed me how and where to set them. This was only to be done on Friday evening and Saturday, and only in the month of January when furs were prime. So at an early age I became a fur trapper.

I was out at the crack of dawn to tend my traps, as I had feelings for the animals. My first night's set held three coons. This was a heavy load for little shoulders and it was with relief that I laid them in the yard and proudly ran into the house to tell my father of my luck. Then came the task of learning to skin out the furs in such a manner that they could be stretched square. At month's end the furs—ten of them—were sent express to a fur dealer in St. Louis, Missouri. When the check arrived

Coon skins. Photo by Herman Betz, 1920s.

it was for $5.00: the first money I had ever had. I had to wait to see the cash until Father made a trip to Clearwater where there was a bank. How wonderful that crisp bill looked to me and how many plans were made on how to spend it. One thing, I was going to have more traps another year. For all the 35 years I spent on the Island I did trap, doing so as humanely as possible. In later years, with a bit more maturity, I was taking out 50 furs each January. This made for a healthier population of animals, as the amount of food was not sufficient to feed the increase in animals.

MORE LESSONS

Here was another school year. A report card in my possession shows I was never tardy and missed only two days of school, no doubt due to very windy mornings. The date is 1906. Different teachers had various ways of opening school. Always a bell was rung, we lined up, boys in one line, girls in the other, and marched to our desks. With one teacher we sang hymns (the school had an organ that the teacher played) then had a short Bible reading. The singing I loved. Mr. L.B. Skinner had made the school a gift of hymn books and pupils chose what they wished to sing.

But this year our teacher was all for physical fitness and instead of Bible reading and singing, there was exercise and deep breathing. We all stood up, swinging our arms around, bending to the left, then to the right, for some long minutes. I was all for it, only I had been up since 3:00 a.m. helping my father with a large catch of fish; then to the house to make breakfast, pack my own lunch, leave one for Father, feed and care for the stock, then wash and dress for school and row the sound, pulling against a northeast wind. Rather than do any explaining, I stood up with the best of them, but inwardly I smiled to myself, thinking how little they do know about this island dweller.

All in all, my few school years were happy ones. There were little trials, mainly because I had only one parent. Local stores did not carry ready-made clothes. School dresses were made by a dressmaker, usually a widow who could sew. My dresses were always "serviceable." How I did wish just once that they could have some lace or other trim. My shoes were ordered from Montgomery Ward's catalog. They, too, had to be "serviceable." Here again, I used to wish for a pair of patent leather pumps with a strap, but instead they were laced to the ankle. Oddly enough, I never made a protest.

There was one thing that did hurt. I was plain-faced to a fault; a ridge of freckles across my nose and cheeks overlapped like shingles, sun-faded blonde hair was pulled back tight in a large braid down my back. No beauty was I, and the girls were quick to tell me so. I took it all with a poker face, but it hurt, and I spilled many tears as I pulled my way homeward across the windy and sometimes rough water.

Myrtle (age nine) with her skiff. (Photo repaired by Lisa Young.)

Father, who had a keen eye, asked me on one of these occasions what was wrong. So I told him. He said, "Sit down Myrtle, we will have a little talk. You are worried because you are plainer than some of the girls at school. Well, I can tell you how you can become one of the most beautiful women in the world." This made me prick up my ears. Father had so much wisdom and often had the simple answer to something that was a riddle to me. After all, I was a little girl at the fairy-story stage. So, to my mind came the idea that there was some magic that Father would tell me about, maybe some potion I could drink. But these were his words: "All you have to do is be kind, thoughtful of others, never say any hurtful words to or about anyone, be helpful and polite. In other words, you treat others as you would like to be treated and you will find that treatment in kind will be returned to you." Well, this gave me something to think about at least, and through the years I've tried to practice Father's teaching.

The other little thorn in the flesh was not quite so painful; I was called the "foreigner's daughter." At first I didn't know what it meant, but from the way it was said, I knew it was not meant as a compliment. This, too, I took to Father. It drew a laugh from him as he explained it to me and then added, "If you are the only foreigner's child, you must be among only American Indians." So that worry, too, went into the background of my mind.

The school yard (an acre) was fenced to keep out roving stock. Noon hour was the high point in the school day. Among the girls there was a social scale, less or none among the boys. So there were separate groups. Lunch time was exchange time, "I'll swap you this for that." Some lunches were in a tin bucket, a cup of cold grits with a fried piece of salt pork on top and a spoon to eat it with. For a drink, there was a pitcher pump with a bucket and dipper. I never heard a child complain of what their lunch contained; each fell greedily to whatever had been packed for them.

Boys played baseball after lunch outside of the school yard. This was off-limits to girls. They played house in a saw palm patch, with a broken orange crate and some bits of china. There were mothers and aunts, and always the littlest member of the school was the baby. This seemed to me a bit dull. I played real house at home. One day some

Photo of Myrtle taken during her last year in school.

of the older girls were watching the boys playing ball when one of the girls spoke up and said, "Why can't we older girls have a ball team?" This met with instant response. So, one of the girls from the country brought a ball and much-used bat to school and we all trooped outside the fence to a cleared spot. The know-hows among the girls marked off the bases and we were playing ball.

To me, this was great fun; to swat the ball and make a home run was very gratifying. I liked action. But our girls' ball team was to be short-lived. Within the week the teacher requested all the girls that had played ball to stay after school as she wished to talk to us. We all were a little nervous and had a feeling of what was coming up. The teacher did not mince words. She said she was disappointed in us, as she had thought we were all young ladies, but our actions had proved otherwise. She asked us to discontinue our ball games. We were all in disgrace and that was the end of our ball playing.

Too soon school years were over and whatever I had of childhood was gone. Eighth grade was the end of the school in Dunedin. Very few of the children would continue their education. We all had a favorite teacher in our last year; it was a Miss Ova Allison, a good teacher and a good friend. On closing day many of us did not rush off, but stayed to talk to her as she gathered up from her desk some few personal things. It was a sad time for me. I would be seeing the friends I had made seldom, if at all, and deep inside me I had a feeling that I should have more schooling. But at last it was time to say goodbye, take one last look at the schoolroom and walk the distance to the dock where my little boat was tied up. Home looked good to me, but I had a feeling there was a world out there that I did not know. Maybe I was sprouting the wings of restless youth.

EQUINOCTIAL STORMS

It was in the month of September; gusts of wind whipped out of the northeast with spats of rain; low, gray puffs of clouds hurried across the sky. The air felt strange. Father said there was to be a bad blow and there were preparations to be made. The skiffs had to be tied securely, extra anchors on the boats moored in the open. Nets were bunched and tied to the net racks. I was to carry in as much dry wood as I could stack by the stove, fill the water bucket and see that the lamps were filled with kerosene and the chimneys polished. The wind increased, the sound of it like an express train; the water in the bayou was covered with white caps and the tide rose at an alarming rate. Night came on early. Slowly the wind moved from south to west. Gusts made the house tremble. I put a scant supper on the table, which we scarcely touched. Just how high would the water come? We knew the fall garden planted in a low spot would be lost to sea water. Looking out the window, only dashes of rain and darkness could be seen. In bed in my garret room, I could hear the wind shrieking in the eaves. At some time I fell asleep and, on awakening at dawn, found the wind had fallen off to only a stiff breeze out of the north. Such a sodden world met my eyes.

The yard was one mass of palm fronds and broken oak limbs. The high water was gone, leaving great piles of trash and much lumber and dock parts, from we knew not where. A few shingles off the roof and the loss of our garden was all the damage we could find, but a big clean-up job was in the yard.

Later I saw many of these storms. Even in the later years when we got weather reports, I could still remember this as my first equinoctial storm (now called a hurricane); and always the signs were the same: that gusty northeast wind with those spats of rain. In the thirty-five years that I lived in the sheltered bayou of Caladesi, there was never any damage done to the property, never any loss of boats or fishing gear.

As soon as some of the storm's debris had been cleared from the yard, I was off to the outer sea beach. There was much brought in and piled in windrows above the normal tide level. Several small battered boats, beyond repair, but with useable hardware, lay in a smother of sea grass and tree branches. Near the water's edge was the boom, gaff and

Henry in high tide after 1921 hurricane, Scharrer Bayou behind him.

heavy canvas sail of a large sailing vessel. It had been chopped loose from the mast, as the wooden mast rings showed axe marks. Not far away was a trunk cabin of mahogany. We never learned if there had been a tragedy and maybe lives lost.

Pitiful, water-soaked, dead sea birds were mixed with the mass of drift; also the bodies of many kinds of fish that the huge waves had thrown on the beach. These would not remain long, as already ghost crabs were busy dragging the smaller fish to their burrows and coons had made an early morning trip, partly eating many. The dead fish had drawn a host of beach-dwelling insects, and sandpipers and turnstones were busy picking these off. When the waves subsided, we would take a skiff around to the beach and collect some of the useable treasures the sea had brought in. I would enjoy turning beachcomber for a day. Much use would be made of these gifts from the sea.

SEA LIFE

There was always so much to look forward to when there was slack time. One thing that was of great interest was to lie belly down on the T-head of the dock, mainly at incoming tide. "Little Dog," a small dogfish, lived under the dock in a pure white left-handed whelk. It had been his home for some time and he was starting to grow out of it. He would back in, but now his head was exposed. Once he could get in all the way. It was great fun to feed him fish scraps whenever fish were cleaned, as he would eat until his sides bulged and he could hardly get into his house. He always seemed ill-tempered, darting out at anything that came near his home with a warning not to trespass. Hermit crabs got knocked to "galley-west." "Big Dog" lived some distance away in a crab burrow that he had taken over. Big Dog was a neat housekeeper with a nasty temper; he fanned the entrance to his home, keeping it clear of everything. The two dogfish did much barking back and forth, answering each other's calls. Maybe it was friendly chit chat. In spite of the sharp spines on the head of the dogfish, they had one enemy, the large Ward's heron. At low tide, the herons searched the grass flats and any dogfish unlucky enough not to have a shelter became heron food.

The homestead dock from Scharrer's Bayou. Myrtle's husband, Herman, built the boat.

Little Dog had for company a row of anemones. They looked like flowers, fed on what the tide brought them and were quick to withdraw if any fish investigated them. Oysters on the dock piles were happy to get bathed in the incoming tide and snapped their shells, throwing streams of water. A small stone crab, busy making a burrow, hurried to the entrance, pushing sand before him with extended claws. At the entrance he would spread his claws and deposit the sand in front of his burrow. This was hard work and he paused to rest each time before going in for another load. A frogfish came by, half swimming, half walking, paused to look things over, then went on. With the tide, clams buried in the sand opened up their keyholes to take in food. Black piling crabs with their square bodies were moving up the pilings out of the water's reach, and a small sheephead was looking over the oysters for one small enough to crush with its mouth full of sharp teeth. Now the fiddler crabs were hurrying out of the grass that they had been cleaning of algae. It would not be safe to be caught in the incoming tide, as there was always a channel bass looking for laggers. The fiddlers would go to their burrows about the high tide mark and await the next low tide.

While I am enjoying all this show of sea life, a small fish with great pectoral fins, looking much like a butterfly, swims by; and a scallop jets in, settling on the bottom for a minute with open shell, as if looking over the territory with its forty blue eyes, then takes off again. It is with reluctance I start to leave. As I get to my feet, out from the edge of the dock there are a bunch of twenty or so silver-sided mullet. They are digging in the sand like pigs, taking in a mouthful and then sieving it out. On a summer spring tide the small killifish comes to lay its eggs (July). The males are decked in gay black and orange; the females in their black and white stripes. There is just one spot they pick; it has flour-like soil at the very edge of the tidemark. The females dig into this, sometimes throwing themselves about the high tide mark. The males follow; in what seems a few minutes they come struggling out of the sand ready to swim away. The eggs will hatch the small fingerlings on the next high spring tide, which will be in two weeks. In another year this will all take place again.

PARTNERS

It was on one of these dock visits that I solved what was to me a mystery and no one gave me the answer. Bay cats (catfish) with their meaty tails cut off clean could often be seen struggling on the water's surface. The bald-headed eagles sat on the tallest of the pines not far from their nest and, spotting these catfish, picked them out of the water. Under their nest was a great pile of remains. The pile was eighteen inches high, the result of many years, as this pair of eagles had built their nest in 1888, the same year that Father had found his Shangri-La. On this morning the tide was at its height. Suddenly a pair of bottle-nosed dolphins (we called them porpoises) came near the dock,

I supposed after a mullet meal. There was a swirl of water as the bottle-nosed dolphins continued on their way, and as the wavelets calmed down I saw a cut, crippled cat; and here came an eagle from his pine lookout to pick it up. So no more mystery. The wise and skillful porpoise knew

Henry's dock and the path leading to his home.

how to cut off the meaty tail and avoid the wicked spines. So the eagle and the porpoise each shared something in common.

OUR WINGED FRIENDS

This pair of eagles were friends and neighbors. Their tall pine nesting tree was no great distance from our home. Eagles as such were shot on sight by the natives, as they were supposed to catch and carry off livestock. During the many years we and the eagles lived in harmony they never caught a small pig or chicken. I say small, as an eagle can get off the ground with no greater weight than four pounds. The food of these eagles was fish, wounded or sick seabirds and now and again a rabbit caught on the mainland, as the island had no rabbits.

Oddly enough, eagles are like pack rats, collectors of articles that are not food nor needed for nest repairs. In their nest were such things as golf balls, torn jackets, old straw hats and work gloves. Many of these things could be picked up on the beach or floating in on the tide. This pair of bald-heads spent the months from the first week in September to the first week in May on the island.

The eagles' nest in a pine tree near the homestead.

Their first duty when they came in September was the repair of their huge nest, which, over the years, became at least eight feet high. Each year pine branches of some size were added to it and always Spanish moss. We would search the September sky for our friends' return, and it was a happy day when they would be seen soaring in circles over the house and their nesting tree. At their arrival, they were noisy and did much calling while flying. They spent some time in their tall lookout tree, sitting side by side.

Mrs. Eagle being a much larger size than Mr. Eagle, they were easy to tell apart. But on the wing their size was not apparent. By January there were little heads sticking above the nest rim. Often there were three eaglets, but one was always much undersized and weak and was probably stomped to death by the larger birds, as three never left the nest at flying size. It was always two husky big black birds, larger than their parents, that took to wing in late March. Some time in the first week of May, the whole family of eagles left. Every once in a while there would be, for a short time, one immature black bird following them back in September, but it never remained long. In the early spring, sometimes before the eagles would leave, the ospreys arrived to repair their nests. There was often more than one pair using the pine woods of Father's land. These fish hawks fished the bayou, mostly for the plentiful grass grunts or mullet.

One story was that the eagle robs the fish hawk of its fish. Like a lot of nature tales, this was not so. It was a game played by the eagle and osprey. It was always played over a body of water. The eagle would be on his lookout perch. Suddenly, out of nowhere, the osprey would appear high in the sky with a fish in its talons. On flapping wings that held it in one place, it would start calling. The eagle would launch himself on powerful wings. The eagle, much the faster flyer, could not make the sharp, fast turns the osprey could. At no time was this an attack by the eagle. The game was to see if the eagle could catch the dropped fish in the air before it hit the water. If he didn't, the osprey won. If the eagle caught the fish in mid-air, the eagle won. The chase would last some minutes. Finally, the osprey would drop the fish when the eagle was at a disadvantage. As soon as the eagle saw the falling fish, he would dive for it with folded wings, grabbing it in his talons, often getting beneath the fish and turning over on his back. If the fish hit the water and sank, it was lost, and the osprey, the winner, did what sounded much like laughter. If the eagle flew off with the fish, neither bird made a sound.

Several times in my wanderings about the location of the ospreys, I would hear one calling close overhead and on looking up would have a small fish dropped to me, usually a grey grass grunt. I always picked up the fish and waved at the bird as a thank-you. The fish, placed near the runways of the coons, would provide a meal for one of them.

A Mr. Brown, a mail carrier in Dunedin for many years, told this story. He was riding his bike along Victoria Drive delivering mail. The Drive is along the water's edge. He became aware of an osprey calling close overhead. When he looked up, the bird dropped a large fish. Mr. Brown found a two-pound pompano lying in the grass. A pretty nice gift!

A cardinal perched on the bird feeder that was designed to foil squirrels and raccoons.

One other large bird nested in the pines. This was the Ward's heron. The nest was a poor excuse, being some sticks laid loosely over the pine branches, daylight showing through the unlined nest. Often the eggs would drop through the poorly-made nests, smashing on the ground. No bird is as gawky and awkward as a baby heron. Straightening out its neck is enough to overbalance it, so many of the little newly-hatched chicks also ended up on the ground. There was always a lot of wing-spreading and beak-thrusting done by the parents at nearby neighbors. As a rule, there would be several nests in the same tree. Sometimes a sudden windstorm finished the nesting season of the Ward's, as all the nests would be blown down.

BIRD-BRAINED?

There were so many bright spots in our day-to-day living that it would be hard to pick out any one thing; we got enjoyment out of very simple incidents. Just such a small thing as an unusually brilliant sunset would make my heart swell with a thankful feeling. A flock of roseate spoonbills would drift in, settling where they could be watched, scooping the mud flats with their spoon-shaped bills. What a picture this brings to mind: such gorgeous colored birds feeding among the plainer white and blue herons.

Just how bird-brained is a bird? When I was walking in the yard a male cardinal flew at me, picking at my clothes, then flying off a pace and coming back to fly against me and pull on a piece of my dress. This little bird was trying to tell me something. As soon as I started to follow him, he flew to a nearby palm tree and alighted where his mate was hanging in some palm fibers in which she had become entangled while gathering them to line her nest. Getting a ladder, I reached the little bird and broke the strong fibers away from her neck and wings, and she flew off unhurt with her happy little mate.

On a windy, rainy night in the spring migration period, a small bird darted in the open door to the hall where we kept shelves of canned goods. As if it had known right where to go, it lit on a shelf and settled itself. Next morning early I thought of the little visitor and knew it would want its freedom. So as soon as the door to the outside was opened, the bird dashed out. Little wildling, I'm glad you found shelter for the night.

Once, a bird fleeing for its life from a Cooper's hawk flew against me then fluttered back of me. The hawk, so intent on its prey, was only a few feet away and hurriedly "put on the brakes" and took off. For the time, at least, the bird was saved by pulling this get-away trick.

OTHER PLEASURES

It didn't need to be nature to make my heart sing. Back from town and a visit to the post office and there would be that wonder of wonders, a new Montgomery Ward catalog (called a "wish book"), something to spend many pleasant evenings going through the pages. Then there was the *Saturday Evening Post*, always with a good adventure story, and the weekly paper from Clearwater had local news of many we knew. Father also took *The Literary Digest* (not published anymore) and *The Scientific American,* which I loved, as I was thirsty for any information. Father was a great reader, and that's how those lamp-lit evenings after supper were spent on such nights as tides or weather kept him from being out with his nets after a fish catch.

Once a month there came a grocery list from Montgomery Ward. This service has long been discontinued, but to folks isolated on farms far from a store, it was a service much used. From this catalog, Father filled in an order sheet, a money order from the post office went off with it and some time later a notice from the freight station would be in the mail, stating that there were a certain number of boxes at the railroad station.

There would be dried fruit, apples, figs, prunes, beans of several varieties, macaroni, a small wheel of cheese, a pretty canister of tea and green coffee berries that had to be roasted to a nut brown in the oven and ground fresh each morning in a hand grinder held between the knees to steady it. If it was near the end of the year and Christmas was in sight, a bag of mixed nuts and a small pail of hard candy would be in one of the wooden boxes the shipment came in.

Then there was the day that one of the boxes contained an Edison phonograph. The records were cylindrical in shape. They were slipped on a smaller cylinder and an arm with a needle was placed on the record. After winding the machine with a key, out of that black record came music. To me it was a miracle. Later we had the flat type of record and a "His Master's Voice" record player. This meant much to me in my young years, and I loved music. So I heard the voices of the great singers of those early years and much opera. What would be the first? *William Tell!* My father, at about this time, taught me to read music and I picked out tunes on a zither and sang the popular music of those days. Among the songs were "Listen to the Mocking Bird," "Suwannee River" and "My Old Kentucky Home." At Christmas time, Father often sang "Silent Night" in German while playing his violin. It is still one of my favorites.

CHRISTMAS AWAY FROM HOME

Christmas meant a fragrant cedar tree with homemade beeswax candles and ornaments saved from one year to another, many of these also homemade. The gifts were simple, and many times they, too, were homemade. But store-bought gifts, though few, were treasures to my eyes. A set of dishes stands out in my mind, so complete with useable little teapot, sugar bowl and creamer. One Christmas I was asked by a school chum to spend Christmas at her home. I thought it would be nice to see how others had Christmas. This friend, Vera Holmes, lived in the country some two miles from town in a huge house with her parents and many older sisters, a brother and small niece. So Father took me to Dunedin where Mr. Holmes and Vera were waiting for me with horse and buggy.

This was the day before Christmas and Father was to be at the dock the day after Christmas to pick me up. Mother and grown daughters were busy in the kitchen. This was a large room separated from the main house by a walkway called a dogtrot. Most Florida homes of any size had this arrangement. It kept the heat of a wood stove out of the main house and had first been used when slaves worked in the kitchens. Vera and I were given the chores of cracking and picking nuts. On Christmas Day, the twelve-foot long table, built of planks and trestles, was loaded with food: great piles of fried chicken, roast

Henry with visitors, probably locals rather than out-of-towners. Notice the beehives.

chicken, pans of stuffing, huge mounds of brown biscuits, baked sweet potatoes and dishes of turnips cooked with their greens. Then there were pies of several kinds and cakes with colored icing.

The women who had cooked the meal did not sit down at the table. They kept busy refilling empty dishes. There were neighbors in as guests. Every space at the table was filled. There was very little conversation, as each person seemed to keep their eyes on their plates, and did the food disappear! After the meal, there was much throat-clearing, some burps and chair-scraping as the men in the group headed for the front porch where they lit vile-smelling pipes, sat and said little. Hip flasks were passed around. The women helped clear off the table. In the kitchen it was a beehive of chatter. One by one the guests drove off in their wagons or buggies. Some had miles to drive to their homes.

Vera and I took a walk to a nearby pond and on the way back drove in the family's milk cow. The weather was chilly. The house had no heat, only a fireplace in Mr. Holmes' bedroom. Vera and I, being the "little ones," were allowed to warm ourselves by it before jumping into a cold bed. This was a big privilege.

Mr. Holmes had a wholesale business of selling shells and other oddities from the sea: small stuffed or dried sea creatures such as sea horses, file fish, the bills of sawfish and colorful sea fans in purple and yellow. Much of this was shipped overseas, Germany being a big market. To Germany went barrels of the white half of the scallop shell. It sent them back to us on satin-lined baskets and made into pin cushions, as every parlor had a whatnot shelf to display odd bits and pieces. No whatnot shelf was complete without something from that faraway, mysterious Florida.

I was glad when the day after Christmas arrived, as I was a little homesick. Mr. Holmes and Vera drove me to the dock where Father was waiting. I'd been given a generous box of cake and I was pleased to have some to share at home with Father. Good-byes and thanks were said and we set sail for the island.

When I entered the house there was a Christmas tree all trimmed in the middle of the room. A great wave of sadness came over me. I had not thought of my father alone on Christmas day, but he had

A picnic under the trees with everyone dressed in their Sunday best, Henry at far right.

thought of me. Right then, though I could not have said the words, I vowed never would I be so selfish again. Under the tree were gifts. One I cherished for years was a sewing kit: all colors of thread, needles, thimble and scissors. All this took place at the age of twelve, and I've never felt more grown up than at that time.

ENTERTAINMENTS AND ISLAND VISITORS

Often, on moonlight nights, groups of young people would arrive at dusk at our home for a cook-out supper. This would almoſt always consiſt of several chickens cut up and cooked in a large iron pot over an outdoor fire. When the chickens reached the near-tender ſtate, rice was added and cooked down. This cooking was always the duty of the men folks. A great pot of coffee was on one side of the fire. The food was served in wooden throw-away plates—no paper plates at that time. Someone, usually the couple or couples that had come as chaperones, supplied the flatware. Some of the party had brought either cakes or pies. Father had built a large table and benches, and cut a ſtack of wood for the cooking; such a happy time, everyone was friendly and laughing. The young couples did much teasing, but they were never rough or unduly noisy. There was no drinking and no smoking, unless it was a pipe of one of the men who were in the chaperone group. After the picnic supper was over, someone in the group would have a mandolin or guitar and we would gather around

Groups of visiting young ladies referred to their camp as "Adamless Eden." Henry was often asked to chaperone when women from Clearwater and Sutherland College came to visit.

Henry after returning from an outing as a fishing guide with string of sheephead.

the cook fire that was now a bonfire and sing. Then it would be time to leave for the sail back to Clearwater.

These are sweet memories of the past. Few, if any, of these folks are still with us. The names still appear in the news—Coachman, Martin, Hart, Tilley—but these are the children of the couples who once so long ago visited and enjoyed a moonlight evening on what they called "Scharrer's Island."

In these faraway days, there was little for the many tourists that were filling the hotels to do. Men went quail shooting, fishing or played golf. For the ladies there were cards and gossip; no roads, no cars. One hired a horse and buggy to visit a nearby town. But water travel was available. Clearwater had charter (sail) boats at the city dock.

Young ladies rest and relax near their beach camp.

Visitors being shown the garden during a tour of the homestead.

There was, across the sound, what was called Shell Island, Clearwater Beach today. Here one could picnic and walk the Gulf-lapped beach searching for its treasure of shells. Anclote Lighthouse, a distance of some fifteen miles and a full day's trip, was often visited.

Nearer and of increasing interest was Hog Island or Scharrer's Island. Here the boatmen brought their fares of the curious and the interested. My father never seemed to tire of showing visitors around his acres of semi-tropic island. When a group would arrive, he would drop whatever he was doing and become a gracious host. Paths had been cleared leading to points of interest.

Visitors assembled at the Indian mound. Henry is second from left. Henry would tell tall tales to entertain his guests—and sometimes even the adults believed him.

The first stop on the walk was our large and well-cared-for garden. There was always much amazement that a garden could be grown on an island. This always struck me as strange. What was so different about an island? Father answered questions, named plants and trees, pointed out birds and especially the nests of the eagles and herons. The Indian burial mounds were a high point in the nature walk. As many of these visitors came from the plush Belleview (later the Belleview Biltmore) Hotel, I met the great and near-great.

In our home, which most of the visitors wished to see, I had been given one corner for my own. There was a little roll-top desk and chair and, plastered on the walls, covers from *The Saturday Evening Post.* These were usually lovely ladies posed with beautiful horses or dogs and were done by an artist named Charles Dana Gibson. Among these, there hung a picture of Sears and Roebuck's new great building in Chicago. At that time there were no branch stores. This picture had been included in one order for free, and such a huge building I had never seen, so up on the wall it went. A gentleman visitor in our home stepped

Henry with Mr. and Mrs. Haines of Pittsburgh.

up to me and, pointing to the picture, said, "I'm Mr. Thorn, the head of that business." No doubt he was as much impressed by seeing his great building hanging on the wall of a pioneer Florida home as I was on meeting him.

Among the names I recall were those of Robert Lincoln (he and my father visited often) and the poet-writer Carl Sandburg. Maybe his visit had something to do with the fact that Lincoln wintered in Clearwater. Much later, Sandburg sent a copy of his *Lincoln, the Prairie Years* to my father. With a dream in my heart that someday I, too, might write, I sometimes got a bit of encouragement, as when Rex Beach said, "You can do it." A shy little islander telling her dream to a writer.

Maybe the greatest thrill of all was hearing Fritz Kreisler play on Father's violin. Then there was a friend who brought Eddie Ricken-backer to visit. After reading in the papers so much about this World War One ace and later of his miraculous rescue in the Pacific, I felt very humble and privileged to meet this fine, well-known figure. And now, just maybe we islanders were different, as had been pointed out by some of the local people.

"... GO TO SCHARRER'S"

Sometimes it seemed that the island house should have been designated as a life-saving station. The word to anyone going out on the water was, "If you get in trouble, go to Scharrer's." We had storm-bound people coming to the place for a few hours to overnight, until

A. J. Grant, mayor of Dunedin, with Henry at the Harp Tree.

Henry with four women at the Harp Tree.

Henry with *Atlanta Constitution* Editor Clark Howell (in black), who gave Henry a gift subscription to the paper. (The third gentleman is unidentified.)

Henry with a visitor sitting in the Harp Tree.

Eleanor and Lee Malone seated in the popular Harp Tree.

Two women visitors pose in the Harp Tree while Henry stands nearby.

some wind or rain storm was over. Coming across the sound in small and overloaded boats, many found themselves unable to make it back to the mainland. So they would arrive at our door for help, shelter and, most times, food. Once, half a dozen men came in late one evening saying they were afraid to try the crossing since the wind had sprung up. They explained they were new to the section and had come down from the Carolinas to pick oranges. Father said he, too, thought it would be unwise for them to attempt a crossing until the wind lessened, so he made them a supper of buckwheat pancakes, sausage and coffee. Spreading large canvas sails on the floor of the main room, they spent the night and were sent off next morning with a repeat of their supper. So over the years many were sheltered, fed and helped.

Once, seeing a schooner anchored off the beach, Father went to find out if they were in trouble. There had been a long stormy spell and at the time the wind had been out of the south, blowing a gale for three days. The palm fronds were parted and twisted on the palm trees; that showed the strength in the wind. The schooner was a Cuban fishing smack. The crew had a story of no fish and now they were running out of food, had no money and would have to return to Cuba with empty fish wells.

Father offered to stake them to groceries and would give them a couple of pigs and some chickens to take on board to butcher later. This was a common practice in the days before refrigeration. Father, with one of the crew members, sailed to town and bought groceries. The crew came to the house, got their pigs and chickens and next morning the schooner had left for the Gulf, the wind having lessened. Some months later, there was a great commotion and loud jabbering at the dock. Here was a ship's longboat and a dozen swarthy men.

The fishermen had returned to pay for all they had received. Also, they were loaded with gifts: ripe mangos, guava paste and for Father, bottles of "vino." For several years this same crew came to our home and bought livestock, honey and fresh vegetables, and they never came without some thank-you gifts. When they did not return one year we wondered if a mishap might have taken place. We never saw them again after that. For years a picture of the crew on the cabin of their smack stood on my Father's desk.

At around two o'clock one morning, there was a noise of a landing and a "hello" from the dock. On being answered, a young man came to the door and asked if it was possible to take him to Dunedin. He gave his name and said he had had word that his father, who lived in Dunedin, was sick. The young man was at Key West. He had boarded a coast freighter, which was laying off in the Gulf waiting for the return of the crew and longboat. So Father rowed the man across the sound in the early morning hours. Such was travel in those early years.

Once there was a very unhappy event. With a strong southeast wind blowing, we noticed a small sailboat headed for the open Gulf. The boat was sailed by a man and his teenage son. They had visited Father many times. We remarked our concern over their taking to the open water in such a gale of wind and then thought no more of it until next morning when the man sailed to the dock and asked if his son was with us. His story was that the boat had capsized at dusk and, the beach seeming close, the boy had said he would swim to it and go to Father's for help. The boy being a strong swimmer, the father gave his consent. He soon lost sight of the swimming figure as night came down, but felt sure he would reach the beach. The tide carried the boat farther off shore but during the night the wind let up and the man was able to right the boat and sail into our place. The boy's body was never found.

On a Christmas week in about 1909, a motor vessel ran aground on the sand bar at Big Pass. Before it could be floated by a high tide, the wind came out of the northwest with great pounding seas and washed the pilot house and upper structures off, at the same time pounding the bottom open. The name of the boat was the *Three Friends* and she had carried a cargo of assorted freight. On the beach came bales of hay and grain along with the wreckage. On the bar where the boat grounded at low tide could be seen canned goods. We picked up many of these cans and it was interesting to open one for a meal and not know if it was canned peaches or baked beans.

The hull finally floated off the bar and came to the inside channel, where it again grounded and became covered with sand. Once before, a ship's hull had washed near the outer beach. This boat had no doubt been wrecked at sea. Lying on its side, only the hull left, the bottom had planks loose from the keel. My father said that the wreck was caused by a jumped mast. In very heavy weather, masts sometimes got unstepped and on going down would loosen the ship's bottom planks. The sea is so beautiful, so powerful and can be so cruel.

LAST RUN TO TAMPA

Now again came the time of year when there was a store of honey, fresh-dug sweet potatoes and wheels of beeswax. So the sloop *Water Witch* was loaded for a run to Tampa. I liked these trips and I didn't. Leaving home even for a short time was always painful to me. There seemed so many things demanding my attention. But it made me feel pride that I could handle the boat and make the meals in the tiny galley. Father said this would probably be our last trip as the nearby towns of Dunedin and Clearwater were fast growing and he had made some connections to dispose of produce.

Photo of downtown Clearwater in 1895. (Courtesy of Florida State Archives.)

With a fair wind, we headed south into the Gulf. Only a ground swell kept the *Water Witch* nodding as her white sails bellowed in the wind. By evening we were well into Tampa Bay and docked early the next morning. Because of waterfront thieves, I spent the time on the boat while Father went into the city to find customers. The beeswax would go to a cobbler's shop where it found a ready sale. Hucksters would buy the sweet potatoes and some of the food stores the honey. The first day and everything was sold, and Father was pleased and maybe a little smug at how well he had done.

It was now blowing a very brisk wind out of the west. Close-hauled, we would get out of the harbor without tacking. Sailing down the bay, we had noticed for some time a speck of a boat being rowed. In heavy wind and seas, it seemed to be no more than holding its own. As we came nearer, we saw the small boat contained only the man at the oars. Father said to come about and we sailed over to him, as we could give him a tow. On luffing up alongside of him, Father asked him to throw us a line. He seemed very tired and said he was headed for his home on Ballast Point, which he pointed out. In no time we had come to the shore where a small building was on the waterfront. The man was profuse in his thanks and asked us ashore, but Father said we would stop another time. The thing that impressed me was a cat sitting on his dock awaiting his master's return, as I knew there was one at the island dock waiting for me.

THE STOVE PIPE INCIDENT

Whenever I was alone (Father would be gone on some errand to town or had taken a party deep-sea fishing) I'd turn to house cleaning to pass the time. The windows would be washed. When they were polished with a newspaper, they showed sun-burnt colors of blue and pink. The wood box would be cleared of chips and piled high with fresh-cut wood and finally the floor would be scrubbed. It would all smell so fresh and clean, and I looked on our home with love and pride.

I'd be glancing out to watch for Father's sails, and that would mean turning my attention to getting a meal ready. Kindling laid in the wood stove, there would soon be a brisk fire and food cooking.

A gallon kerosene can was in the kitchen, used to fill the lamps, and often if Father lit the fire I would see him first pour a small amount of kerosene on the kindling, then light it. This would make the fire burn much quicker. Now on many occasions, as I watched him do this, he warned me never to do it. Seems some things were all right for grown-ups to do but were out-of-bounds for children. A glance out the door; the boat was nearly at the dock. So to hurry the fire just this once I'd pour on a little kerosene. As I did so, a little smoke seemed to come up from the kindling. I touched a match to it. There was a flash, a boom and stove lids flew in all directions. The stove pipes parted and came down on the floor with a clatter. Black soot filled the air and drifted down like snow. The fire was sending up puffs of smoke that were filling the room.

I was aghast, but started pouring dippers of water on the fire, which went out. At this time, Father walked in and, looking things over, said, "I see you have done what I told you not to do." I was speechless among the wreckage I had caused. But Father calmly picked up the stove pipes and replaced them while I did the same with the stove lids. Then I lit the fire and soon had an omelet, hash brown potatoes and coffee on the table that first had to be cleared of the rain of soot. The rest of the day I spent clearing up and feeling very guilty. No more was ever said of the incident. I'd learned my lesson.

Henry on the front porch of his home. During his 44-year residence on the island, many people benefitted from his hospitality and helpfulness.

Small sailboat anchored in Caladesi waters.

Four

RICH OBSERVATIONS

On calm evenings, with an incoming tide, I enjoyed half-drifting, half-paddling very quietly to a point where the tide, rushing in from the Gulf, divided, some racing down the channel, some pouring into the bayou. Here also the sea life split, some following the deep channel, others entering the bayou, all searching for food. In the dark there was little to see but much to hear. The snapping sound came from shrimp and the splashes were lady fish feeding on the shrimp. Snorts and grunts came from channel bass. A "whoosh" and tail splash was a playful bottle-nosed dolphin. Something in the deep water took to the air and came down with a flat splash, a leopard ray. Then there was the outline of a floating form. This was an old-timer going over the same route twice each twenty-four hours: a huge loggerhead turtle, his head as large as a water bucket. Some nights the phosphorescence was so bright that each moving creature could be seen. On tiring of this parade, and with as little noise as possible, I would paddle across the channel to a large white sand bar. Here would be the outline of a fair-sized shark swimming near the bottom. On being struck at with an oar, it would scatter in all directions, only to take the shark form again. Some type of very wise little fish. How did they learn this shark trick? If it was in the later summer, near the mangrove edge a heady, exotic fragrance filled the air. This was the bloom of the buttonbush. Large white spots high in the mangrove tops were moonflowers. And so back to the dock and the comfort of my garret room. These trips stand out in my mind as being more entertaining than the movies I've seen.

THE ISLAND FARM

Because of the excessive poachings, Father had decided to give up hog-raising. I was glad for two reasons; I'd had a silent fear that there might be a tragedy, for the poachers all carried guns and there had been some very angry words exchanged when they had been found slaughtering a hog. The second reason was that more and more, as I grew older, I found helping with the butchering very distressing. To kill the pigs after seeing them grow from cute piglets, and having fed and cared for them, was to me almost like turning against a friend. The colonies of bees had grown to seventy-five hives. These, with the proceeds from net fishing, were making good returns, and I could help with both the bees and the handling of the nets. As for a little personal income, there was a flock of hens and the sale of fryers. This Father left up to me. What I made above the cost of feed was my spending money. Also, it supplied the table with chicken and eggs. A large garden was supplying vegetables. Planting, weeding and cultivation was my part. Father prepared the soil, turning it over with a hand plow. As I was given a free hand in ordering seeds, there was little we didn't grow and everything new was tried out. My two favorites were sweet corn and Irish potatoes. Visitors were always shown the garden and marveled that such a fine garden could be grown on an "island." Most visitors went away with their choice of vegetables. The pantry shelves had pickles of many kinds and canned tomatoes. This was before pressure cookers and I did not can the non-acid vegetables. A shrike or butcher bird lent much help in the garden, far more than the poisons used today. As soon as anyone came to the garden to work or gather vegetables, this little bird came flying to perch on a near fence post. Its sharp eyes could

Farm equipment and beehives at the homestead.

spot any worm or insect disturbed and it would fly down, snatch up a cutworm or grub, hurry to impale it on a barbed wire, and fly back to watch for another.

BANDING BIRDS (1920)

It was around this time that I learned about banding birds for the Fish and Wildlife Service. I applied for and was granted a license. This was a most interesting and rewarding project.

The bands of metal, each numbered and of sizes to fit the various-sized birds, were placed on the birds' legs. A record was kept of the kind of bird, age if known, where banded and date. This was for both migrant birds and residents. In the trap, which was a cage baited with food, other banded birds turned up, many times from distant states. It was a thrill to band a migrant one year and find the same bird a year later in a trap. The records of all banded and recovered birds were sent in to the Fish and Wildlife Service. Banding, besides showing the travels of a bird, also proved its age. A mockingbird that nested each year in a grapefruit tree in the yard had been banded as a fledgling and was twelve years old when caught by a sharp-shinned hawk. The sharp-shinned and Cooper's hawks were very destructive to bird life. They were migrating but delayed their departure far too long to suit me. The little, friendly birds that visited the feeders suffered most. Far better than bird feeders is the planting of fruit-bearing trees and shrubs. This gives birds both food and protection.

Henry loved the birds on the island. It's said that the birds would come when he whistled.

THE NEIGHBORS

It was about 1912 that we heard we were to have neighbors. This was big news. A Mr. Goss was taking the ninety-acre homestead that joined Father's property on the north side. This was not as wooded, being grown more to palms and low bushes. Father had mentioned several times that I might homestead this acreage, but I had not reached the age to do so and had shown little interest in the idea. Mr. and Mrs. Goss had a comfortable, small frame house built and moved in. As they had no sheltered landing for their boat, they used our dock. So we saw quite a lot of them. They had no intention of making a permanent home on the island, only to obtain the title to the land. The Homestead Law had been changed and instead of five years residence, only three were now required. The Gosses met all the requirements, such as establishing a livable house, clearing land and planting. They had a home garden, raised flocks of chickens and set out a small grove of limes. Shortly after moving to the island, Mrs. Goss obtained work in Clearwater, staying with other members of the family and only spending weekends at their island home. The Gosses were good neighbors and we helped each other in different ways, shared produce and had pleasant visits and meals at each other's homes. We were sorry when the three years were up and they obtained

View of the Scharrer's home taken from the dock. A party of visitors is taking their leave. A small child, perhaps Myrtle, stands by the house and watches their departure.

title to their land and moved back to the mainland, where Mr. Goss went into the customs office in Tampa. Vandals soon made a shambles of the Goss home, finally burning it down. The grove of lime trees was engulfed in brush and soon died from lack of care. In a few years nature had removed all signs of the clearing. Today, the home of one of the Caladesi Park Rangers stands where the homesteader's frame house once stood.

AWAY FROM HOME (1912)

Maybe I was at the restless age because I, too, left my island home for a short stay on the mainland. For years we had friends who spent the winter months in Clearwater, a Mr. and Mrs. Bass. They came to the island often, he for a day's fishing, while Mrs. Bass just enjoyed a walk in the woods and later would put up a hammock and rest. Their household consisted of a handyman to run their motor boat and drive their car, a nurse-companion for Mrs. Bass and a cook. These they always brought with them on their outings to our place. The cook was a farm girl from Pennsylvania of about my age, named Rosa. We became close friends and spent many pleasant hours together. She told

Myrtle with Mr. and Mrs. Bass in their red Packard. An automobile ride was a special occasion for her.

me of her life on their farm with her two sisters and parents, while I told her of mine, so very different. One day Mrs. Bass asked me if I wouldn't like to spend some time at their home where, as she said, I could help with the cooking and housekeeping and get to go around some with Rosa. Mrs. Bass said that she would pay me wages. This all sounded so wonderful to me, that without asking my father's consent I said I would like to do this very much. So for the winter months of one year I became a girl Friday to Rosa. No doubt I learned much, but as time went on I also felt guilty at having left Father, and at times a bit homesick. The lovely Bass home lacked something; I never felt as comfortable as in my island home, simple as it was. So when spring came and the family left for their

Myrtle with Mrs. Bass, a thoughtful employer.

Northern home, I was glad to return to my duties with my father.

Mr. and Mrs. Bass were wonderful, kind and thoughtful people. They treated their servants like family members. Rosa and I were given tickets to a movie (silent) each Saturday. On Sunday afternoons we went for a drive in the red Packard car. A limited drive because there were few roads. Our favorite was to go into the grounds of the Belleview Hotel. There was a wealth of flowers planted along all the walks and the grounds were beautiful; an oddity was a double-headed sabal palm. We felt quite elegant in our dusters, with veils tying our hats down. Rosa, having married, did not return the following fall, but all through the years we kept in touch with letters until her death many years later.

SPANISH ARTIFACTS

With a little free time, I often got into a skiff and followed the shoreline, picking up driftwood for the wood stove. I'd heard my father say that there were the graves of two Spaniards on Clearwater Island, at that time called Shell Island. The graves were supposed to be under the only pine tree on the island. The location of the tree was very close to the edge of the deep water channel that ran close to the shore at this spot. Deep water ran up to a small beach. On landing, I saw bricks near the low tide mark. They no doubt were ballast out of a ship. Then I found a piece of heavy chain and the blade of a machete. Soon I came on half of an unglazed jar. This was later sent to the Smithsonian Institute and they said it was a 15th century olive jar. It would seem that a ship had pulled in here and remained for some time. I thirsted for information and wished I had a knowledgeable person to give me answers. The story of the graves was that two Spaniards had been killed in a fight and were buried in their full armor. As there was much yellow fever at that time, my father felt that this might have been a fishing boat and some members of the crew had died. But in recent years a Spanish stirrup was found on nearby Caladesi Island and fishermen do not carry horses. Now this spot where I made my finds has been filled in. It is a swanky residential section. Someone has the graves of two unknown men under their well-kept lawn. The artifacts which I found have been lost over the years.

Henry with his binoculars atop the lookout ladder.

As boat motors became available, Father had replaced sail with motor. It was not long before I had my own small skiff with a one-cylinder motor. I was learning about motors the hard way, by experience. The skiff still carried a pair of oars and a pole so a balky motor didn't strand me. Even the bottle-nosed dolphins liked to play around the little boat to show how much faster they could swim. A favorite spot for them to gather was where there was a division of the tide, half-way between Big Pass and Little Pass. In this location, as I was returning home from Clearwater, a young dolphin jumped across the little skiff, looking at my startled gaze with big horse eyes as it crossed the boat. All I could think was that I was glad it had cleared the boat! I never heard of one doing this before.

So sails were something in the past, and as time went on I missed them. Even looking out in the Gulf I saw the smoke from steamers more often now than the sails of two and three-masted schooners that passed hull down in former years. It might be of interest to note that gasoline was twenty cents a gallon. A five-gallon can lasted me a month for the possible twice-a-week trips into either Dunedin or Clearwater.

HOLIDAYS

We took note of holidays. The Fourth of July was a big day in both Dunedin and Clearwater. Dunedin went in for an outdoor picnic held in the little park on Main Street and Bayshore Drive. Everyone brought a covered dish, each housewife trying to outdo the other, and the long tables groaned with fried chicken, salads and pies and cakes. The highlight of the gathering was a baby-judging contest. Baby buggies were decorated with colored crepe paper or flowers and the little ones were in their finery. Small girls begged to push the

Women participating in a Washington's Birthday Parade, St. Petersburg, February 22, 1918.

carriages while beaming mothers looked on. The ladies of the church had freezers of homemade ice cream for sale. It was not unusual to see a child without the price of a dish of ice cream, the whole sum of 15 cents, looking longingly at others being served. But always some kindly soul would reach into his pocket, and it is doubtful if any child went without.

Clearwater's Fourth, it being the larger town, was a little different. Still the picnic lunch, but there were contests for the children, such as sack races. The men had what they called a jousting race; mounted on horseback and armed with a lance, they rode at full gallop along a row of posts and tried to gather rings that hung from the arms of the posts. In the afternoon there was a baseball game, followed by a dance at night. I guess my interest was in the wonderful food, surely not in the long-winded speech some official gave before the lunch was served.

THE THANKSGIVING GUESTS

On Thanksgiving I took pride in making a meal, the products coming from what we raised. There was baked chicken, stuffing, sweet potatoes, mashed turnips, peas, salad and pumpkin pie. We usually had several guests who arrived by boat. One year we had not invited anyone and I thought it was just going to be Father and I. When the meal was ready, Father walked in with two very rough-looking men. I was surprised. It seems these two had been camping overnight on the beach and were making their way in a small boat to Tampa. Such a show of good manners I never saw. They scraped and bowed when entering the house and were smiles from ear to ear. I guess I showed my resentment; at least I'm afraid I did. Rather than sit at the table, I tended table. Coffee cups needed filling fast and piles of hot biscuits disappeared as if by magic. Coffee was poured in saucers and noisily drunk, food was shoveled in on the blades of knives. My father had a hard time repressing a wide smile, as he knew I did not like crude table manners. Then the men told their story. It turned out they were brothers. They both had farms in Suwannee County, but due to a long drought and other disasters common to farmers, there had been no money crops. With farming over until spring, the two brothers had decided to go to Tampa where they hoped to get employment either on construction jobs or at the dry docks. Not having train fare to spare, they were making the trip in a small open boat that could be sailed or rowed. Grown sons had been left at home to look after the women folks. The boys would hunt, fish and trap to help supply food, and as the brothers said, with two mouths less to feed it would be easier. They mentioned their trip along the Gulf Coast had not been easy, as there had been headwinds, rain and cold. Sometimes they had been refused permission to camp overnight and had spent cold, cramped, wet nights in their small boat. They remarked that ours had been the only friendly hand extended to them and thanked us no end. So now my attitude changed on hearing their story, and as they were leaving I passed them a box with the half chicken left from the meal, baked sweet potatoes, a loaf of homemade bread and a jar of jam. "Thank-you, little lady, thank-you so much," rang in my ears as they headed for the dock and took off in their boat. Maybe I learned something about Thanksgiving that day. Also I felt much ashamed of the glum face I had put on; that was a valuable lesson. I knew it had been a pleasanter day because shared and about this I felt good. Our meager supper that evening seemed to taste extra good.

CHRISTMAS PREPARATIONS

Christmas was looked forward to and a lot of preparation was done. I baked German Christmas cookies, called Springerlies, flavored with anise seeds. Any tin container was turned into a cookie jar, colorful paper was pasted on the outside and cut-outs added. Then there were jars of pickles and jellies to gaily wrap. As no housewife of those days ever did housework without an apron, these I also made. In earlier years, when Father kept hogs, there were smoked hams and bacon. Now Father had jars and pails of honey to give. One family we always remembered with a gift liked nothing as much as oysters, so they received a bushel of oysters in the shell and a quart of opened ones. The gifts we got were of a kind: cane syrup and sometimes a crock of homemade butter. No one bought gifts in those days, as money was scarce, and outside of toys for children few gifts were available. Children often received homemade gifts: wagons for boys, maybe a wooden gun; girls got rag dolls. There was always a tree in our home and beeswax candles on it. We often had dinner on Christmas day with friends on the mainland, but those times when we had dinner guests on the Island always seemed the happiest to me. The fragrant cedar Christmas tree, the cheery warm wood fire and the smell of baking food—what memories it calls up so many years later.

THE MELON PATCH

One year we had a large patch of watermelons. They were the largest we had ever grown and there was hope of finding a sale for them. Then, as they ripened, each one was found with a hole cut in it and the insides scooped out. So traps were set, but to no avail, as they were dug out and thrown, and the melons kept being destroyed. A night trip with barn lantern disclosed nothing. In town one day Father mentioned to a friend who often came coon hunting on the island about the crop loss. This friend said he would let Father have a good coon hound on loan. At the time we were without a dog. The man said to just tie "Trailer" near the field of melons and that would take care of the problem. Sounded simple. So the big brown hound, after being fed a good supper, was taken to the garden, tied to a long rope by his collar and given some feed sacks as a bed.

During the night I listened to hear the dog bark but heard nothing. Early the next morning I hurried to the garden, planning to untie the dog and take him to the house for a well-earned meal. On approaching the garden, something looked wrong. The dog did not raise his head on my call to him. Going up to where he lay, I found him dead in a welter of blood. The larger part of the melon patch was trampled down. I hurried back to the house to tell Father. He could hardly believe me. It seems that just by chance Trailer must have gotten hold of a very large coon and the coon had sunk its teeth in the dog's neck, cutting a vein that caused him to bleed to death. We felt very bad and it was hard to report to the dog's owner the death of a valuable animal. Trailer's owner said he was going to teach some very bold coons a lesson. So he brought his pack of hounds over to the island one moonlight night. Friends came to join in the hunt and there was much boasting, laughter and talk of what would happen to any number of coons. But the night's hunt was more hound baying and shouts of men, as only two coons were treed and shot. Wise in the ways of men and dogs from much hunting, the coons would head for the water-covered mangrove land and scatter and dogs would soon lose the trails and tire of climbing over and around the roots and mangrove limbs. So the watermelon patch was forgotten for that season.

WILD PETS

Father very much objected to taming and making pets of wildlife. He said to do so would only lead to their death at the hands of someone with a gun or club. He said to feed them made them unable to care for themselves once the source of food was not forthcoming. As time went on, I found he was correct. But I kept wanting something besides the domestic stock. So besides a pet king snake and

Myrtle and Teddy the raccoon.

a spadefoot toad, I had two coons raised from eight-week-old cubs. They had a spacious wire pen with a sleeping shelf. This was a male and female from the same litter, named Betty and Teddy. Betty never became tame, growling and biting each chance she got, while Teddy became just a big bundle of lovable fur. He liked nothing better than to curl up in my lap; as he grew to weigh eighteen pounds, this was a lap-full. The average weight of a wild coon is twelve pounds. Turned out of the cage, he would follow like a dog and to my surprise did not bother the chickens. The one thing I could teach him about getting his own food was to take him to the shore where he would dig for fiddler crabs, a favorite food. He was always ready and willing to go back into his cage when I became tired of his fiddler digging or had other tasks waiting to be done. This pair lived in captivity for twelve years. When turned loose, Betty took off, never to be seen again. Teddy made his home close by and could be seen at his fiddler digging in daylight hours. Wild coons feed mainly at night and that was Teddy's downfall, as someone spotted this huge tame coon and put a bullet in him.

ANOTHER HOMESTEADER

A fifty-four acre homestead, the last one on the island, had been taken up by a Mr. Zimmerman. This land was on the far north end of the island, nearly six miles from our home. In this acreage there was some very good farm land. A large family of boys helped their father, often staying on the place alone. Mr. Zimmerman was a well driller by trade and often was called to drill wells far from home. As I had gone to school with the Zimmerman boys, those that might be at their island home often rode down on horse-back to have Sunday dinner with us. I was not flattered in any way by their visits as I realized they were not visiting because of me, but because there was a good meal to be had. Father liked the boys and always welcomed them, and it was nice to have guests to share a meal. Also, Mr. Zimmerman, whom I liked a lot, had given me permission to ride the horses he kept on the island at any time.

All my life I'd longed for a horse. I'd had a taste of riding as a tiny child with my mother. Her horse had long been sold. Once, when I had asked my father about having a horse, he had remarked that we would have little use for one, and I knew that was the answer. He did provide me with a horse many years later, or maybe I should say he provided the means with which I got a horse. The Zimmermans remained only as long as it took to prove up on their land. It seemed no one wanted the inconvenience of island living or the isolation, so Father and I remained the only permanent settlers.

SWIMMING DOG

On a shopping trip to Clearwater we saw something thrashing the water, it was like nothing I'd seen before; what looked like a black head was above the water. When we sailed over to it, it proved to be a large, very tired dog. Pulled on board by the scruff of his neck and his own scrambling, he collapsed in the cockpit. What was a dog doing swimming in the middle of the sound? From his tired appearance,

Visitors sitting around the picnic table, with Henry (far left), and Myrtle (right), holding a black puppy. She loved animals and had pets throughout her life.

he could not have swum much farther. He showed no inclination to leave the boat while we were moored at the Clearwater dock. So Blackie, as we called him, went home to the island with us. He was well-mannered, no trouble to keep and always seemed very appreciative of his pan of food.

Time went on and it just seemed we had a dog, until about six months later two young men came and said they were leaving for a trip to south Florida and wanted their dog. It seems they were from a fishing crew that had been living on a nearby island. The dog had swum after their boat and they claimed they saw us pick the dog up, so knew he was all right and had just not gotten around to claim him. Blackie showed he recognized the men but showed no great desire to go with them. We had the dog long enough to become attached to him, so having him taken away made me feel very sad.

SUN OVER THE SOUND

Water trips often had some incident of interest. One spot in a side channel was the home of a green turtle; his head would always pop up in this one section. One fall it was a "V" of blue geese on their flight to their wintering grounds. A flock of eight bald eagles, soaring high overhead during their migration south in early September was a rare sight. A bottle-nosed dolphin was seen trying to get her dead little calf to breathe; she kept shoving it to the surface. Watched for some time; it seemed she was not willing to give up the hopeless task. The sea folks, too, have their tragedies.

SHARKS

On an out-tide with a storm brewing, I saw a lot of splashing and commotion in some deep mud holes in the grass flats. Fins and tails of large sharks were coming out of the water. I was in a small rowing skiff and wanted to see what was taking place, but each time I approached the disturbance, a large shark would come out of the mud hole and head for the skiff; as soon as I retreated, the shark would go back to the deep hole. After a few tries at getting close, each time being challenged, I decided that I did not want an encounter with an angry shark and continued on my way home. Now again I had no answer to this puzzle. Do sharks by chance have a mating time? If so this may be the answer to their odd behavior.

In all the years spent on and around the water, only once did I have an encounter with a shark that might have ended in disaster. Outside of the main Gulf beach there was a large barrier bar, with a possible hundred feet of water between the bar and the main beach. At high tide the water depth would have been about four feet in most places. The bar was a fine shelling spot. One high tide I was wading on the white sand bottom to the outlying bar, the water up to my arm pits, when I became aware of a six-foot shark taking a lot of interest in my feet. It was noon, the sun overhead. I cast no shadow in the water and each time I took a step the sand was stirred up so my two feet resembled flounders moving over the bottom. The shark would make a swirl towards my feet, then retreat to a distance, then return. There was nothing I could think to do but keep heading for the high, dry barrier bar, and I can say, as the shallow water appeared it was a relief to see the shark go back to the deep of the nearby channel.

WEATHER

To us who made a living partly from the sea and who were dependent on weather almost as a lifestyle, whether it would blow and rain the next day was of importance. My first notice of such was in 1899 when my Mother told me to go on the lee side of the house and watch the snow (that's right, *snow*) flakes come down. Tiny bits of white dancing in the air currents. There were icicles hanging from the roof edge, so there had been rain before the snow. Over the years there were tropical storms, high tides, lashes of hail and droughts, and once, in about 1907, a spell of rain that lasted for nearly two weeks. In that time there was hardly an hour that there was not at least a drizzle. The lack of dry wood for the cook stove and the need to bail boats for hours was not soon forgotten. A long drought followed by an excessive high tide killed many oaks and pines growing near the shoreline, as the water-hungry trees took up the salt water. Frost was a rarity, as we were surrounded by water always warmer than the air.

Chickens in the flooded homestead yard after about two weeks of rain.

The rare times there were frosts was when cold hung on for some days and the tides remained low. In real cold weather the tides do not rise enough to cover the grass flats. Fish, turtles and other sea life suffer. In the rare real freezes that take place, as a rule years apart, hundreds of pounds of dead fish of all kinds are stranded in shoal water and die. The fish-eating birds gorge on these stranded fish. It is a windfall for them; coons wade out at dusk to get their share.

FISHERMEN

There was a style of life going back to the Spanish days, until the first Florida boom, that could not exist today. These were first called fish ranches, later fish camps. Any dab of above high-water-mark land on an island was apt to have a shack and net spreads. The only requirement was that there must be deep enough water close to float a shallow-draught skiff. The net men came and went. The range was mainly from St. Joseph Sound to the Thousand Islands. Fish crews in this section were sure the fishing was better to the south; those in that section thought it must be better north. So there was much packing up and moving. Living quarters, mostly one room, built out of lumber gathered along beaches, were taken apart and loaded on skiffs. What household goods there were, generally consisting of a stove, cook-ware, bedding and a few personal things, were loaded up, and they were off to greener pastures, often to return in a few months. One type of building was an open framework covered with palm fronds. This made a snug shelter and was quickly erected. Shutters were used instead of windows of glass. A door often was a frame covered by a piece of canvas. More often than not, whole families lived this way. If there were children, there was little chance for them to go to school. Boys learned to handle boats and nets at an early age and little girls copied their mothers, gathering wood, cooking seafood, maybe gathering oysters, clams and scallops. Those fortunate enough to have more than a spit of land often had gardens and chickens. These itinerant fisher-folks were not looked on with much favor by the mainlanders. They were said to be light-fingered and in many cases were.

As the two sources of money were either farming or fishing, many land owners turned from growing crops to fishing, or at least joined a fish crew during the fall season when mullet were schooling. Gill nets were not much in use; deep seines with a pocket were used to surround the schools of fish that came near a deep water beach. It took a crew of several men to haul in these heavy nets with their load of thrashing fish. These were the days of men and muscle. No motors to make a task easier. A stout man was required on the oars of the seine boat, as the schools of fish did not linger.

Today it is a far cry from those long ago days of commercial fishing. Now motors take the place of manpower. The price paid to fishermen in the 1800's was one cent apiece regardless of weight. Here in 1981, red roe mullet are bringing 50 cents a pound, so one three-pound fish makes the same return that a hundred and fifty once did by count. The day of the old-time fisherman is long gone. Where their small shacks stood, the land has been filled in and beautiful homes with lovely semi-tropic plantings stand today.

ON THE NET SPREADS

There was much repair work on fishing gear. Nets got torn by large fish breaking through or crabs becoming entangled and trying to chew their way out. Sharks had long ago learned that the sound of a net being put out meant easy picking. Grabbing a gilled fish, they would take a mouthful of webbing and leave a large hole. Early I learned to mend nets, as it was something I could do while Father was at tasks I could not handle. Hours I spent standing and leaning over the net spreads. As the spreads were built over the water, be it high or low tide, a parade passed beneath me. Always there were the hermit crabs. These busybodies were always putting on a show. As they never seemed to be satisfied with the cast-off shell they lived in, much of their time was spent looking for a new dwelling. The favorite shell was the plain tulip, being both strong and light. But there were never enough of those to go around, so many hermits had to make out with shells that were heavy to drag around, such as the fighting conch, or the thin paper shell that did not give much protection. The dandy of the lot would

Net spreads on the beach at a local fish camp. (Courtesy of Dunedin Historical Museum, Malone Album.)

have a Scotch bonnet. Crabs outgrew their shells and were to be seen in spiny star shells and the large ones often had a left-handed whelk. One day I was at the spreads when an empty tulip shell rolled around in the tide. Soon a hermit with a smaller shell noticed it and started looking over what seemed to him like a more fitting home. First he stuck his feet in it, then part of his body. It met with instant favor and he rolled the shell over until it was in a position so that he could pull out of his old shell and back into the new home. While he was intent on all this, several of his kind had joined him, and he was kept busy pushing them away. The transfer had to be made quickly, as his soft body was a tidbit many passing fish would relish. Once settled in his new shell, he took off, leaving the old shell for someone it would fit.

Because I was quiet and moved little on the over-water net spread, many of the wading birds passed beneath me. A little blue heron spent minutes standing very still, its gaze on a certain spot, then a quick stab, and a minnow that thought it was well-hidden in some sea grass became heron food. On the edge of the water, a Florida clapper rail leads four newly-hatched black chicks. They are hunting for tiny fiddler crabs and are finding a rich harvest, as there are thousands of the small crabs, they, too, searching for food. Soon a black-crowned night heron comes stalking by; the rail takes her young into a shore-side thicket, as the night heron is not choosy as to food and would relish a rail chick. A teeter-tailed sandpiper bobbing along the shore seems to find nothing to its liking and takes off, whistling as it flies. So the time passes fast as I mend; the tide has come in and the sun is low in the west. It is time for chores on the land and a supper to cook for Father and me. The days are never long enough to finish all the tasks, but there will be tomorrow. The dog, Gypsy, has been lying on the dock waiting for me and she joins me in my round of duties. A cool, damp wind is coming in off the Gulf and the fire in the wood stove while supper is cooking will be welcome.

NORTHWESTER—THE STRANDED FISHERMEN

A gale came out of the northwest with gusts that make the house tremble. So tomorrow I will comb the beach for the treasures the sea has brought in. There will be shells of every kind and color and other sea creatures caught by the pounding waves. The sad sight will be the bodies of small land birds; they have been caught far offshore in their migration flight and the dashing rain and heavy wind have driven them into the rough water. Sometimes there is a harvest of useable lumber carried away from some shore by the extra high tide these storms bring. In the morning the yard is a litter of dry palm fronds the wind has whipped off; the dry stems breaking sound like pistol shots. A treat during the storm's peak was to hear the wild cry of a loon that had taken shelter in the bayou. These birds spend the winter months offshore in the open Gulf. Rarely coming to the beach to slide themselves up on the shore for a short period, these birds cannot walk; their feet are placed aft, much like a ship's propeller. Thank-you, loon, for your wild cry in the stormy night; may you return to your nesting ground on a northern lake and you and your mate with a nest in the reeds hatch out downy chicks, that your voice never be silent down through the coming years. I'm short-changing my chores this early morning that I may reach the beach before flood tide. Each tide changes and rearranges the shore and its contents, taking back some, covering others with sand.

A photo of visitors taken on the island. Myrtle is on the right with her hand on her hip.

But on this morning my looked-forward-to trip was delayed. For hardly had I finished clearing up from breakfast when comes a chorus of "Hello, there." Four rough-dressed men have come down the woods path to the house. I can see my father knows them, as he answers their call. After talking a minute he asks them into the house and introduces them to me by first names. There are John, Jim, Bill and Eric, all men in their 30s. They explain that the night before, they had come up from Indian Rocks, some miles south of us, with their nets to put in a "stop" (a method of fishing now unlawful). With the storm, the tide had not come in, so they had been unable to pick up their nets or float their skiffs. They had spent the time cold, wet and without food. So here it was again, "Go to the Scharrers'!" Father asked me to set places at the table. He stoked up the stove and went about making his famous buckwheat pancakes. He called them flapjacks. A big pot of coffee was soon brewing. Father's pancakes were made in an iron skillet and were plate-size, drenched with honey and butter and washed down with a hot cup of coffee; he considered them a "cure-all." No matter if you were lost, cold, wet or just plain hungry, you got buckwheat pancakes. With hot coffee before them, it was not long before the men were joking and laughing over their plight. As it was warming up, the tide would come in and they could collect their nets and boats and be away by noon. I thought of their families at home, not knowing why husbands and fathers had not returned. But that is ever the way with men "who go down to the sea." Some weeks later, these men, with their families, came up to our home with bountiful picnic baskets of the usual mound of fried chicken, bowls of potato salad and, what was always a big treat for me, layer cakes with gooey icing. There were a dozen children in the party, yelling and running around in circles, ſtirring up the duſt. I'm sure they thought me odd that I did not join them, but to me it seemed aimless. But it was a pleasant time, and Father and I thought it a very nice return for what we had done for the men.

SOUNDS ACROSS THE WATER

We were a mile-and-a-half across Saint Joseph Sound from the neareſt town, Dunedin, yet we heard much of the town's aĉtivities. When the wind was from the eaſt, there was the lowing of a family cow, the barking of a dog, often hammering. The train whiſtles (and in those days they were ſteam whiſtles, now they are air) had such a different sound, so melancholy; it brought up thoughts of many kinds. The sounds I liked beſt were the church bells on Sunday morning and Wednesday evening. As they rang out I would pause, close my eyes and say a little prayer of thanks. I knew how fortunate we were to have health and a happy life. My mother had spoken of that great man Jesus so much to me and I was never allowed to go to sleep without getting on my knees by my bed and saying a prayer, even if it was

View of Caladesi Island (along the horizon) from the dock in Dunedin. (Plant Railroad publicity photo, courtesy of USF Library Special Colleĉtions.)

only the "Now I lay me down to sleep" as a tiny child. Father was a great Bible reader and tried to interest me in doing the same. He did not believe in doing any work on Sundays, but would spend the day reading. For me, as Sunday was a free day, I usually took a long walk over the island, often going to the far north end (now Honeymoon Island). To me there was so much to see. My faithful companion, Gypsy, would be right by my side and often drew my attention to things I would not have noticed, as she was using her nose and eyes. We sometimes surprised a family of coons feeding on some ripening wild fruit. Mother coon would rush off, leaving her three or four youngsters clinging to limbs. No doubt she did not go far, and often as the dog and I walked away, we would see the young start to feed again, so they could not have suffered much of a scare. I would return from these trips tired but feeling enriched by all the little sights nature had shown me. It would be evening on my return from a long walk, and there were small duties to do and an evening meal to prepare for Father and me.

HERO, THE PIGEON

Small incidents gave me much pleasure, as when one morning I saw a pigeon in the yard. Never before had I seen a pigeon on the island. This could have been someone's valuable bird that had become confused or lost. It wore a metal band on one leg and a colored band on the other. When I threw it some grain it ate, then flew off but was back again after some hours. As time went on and the bird remained with us, I got it a mate and built a dovecote and they were soon busy nest building. In those past years, many boys raised pigeons and found a ready sale for the squabs, or young. I enjoyed seeing these pigeons in flight and liked their faithfulness to their nestlings. But when winter came on and the hawks (Cooper's) moved in, my pigeon raising was over, as the hawks spent all their time catching or attempting to catch the last one. The original bird, whom I'd named Hero, came in on foot, having a broken wing and body injuries, yet he had made his way back to his nest site. My pigeon experience makes me think of another disaster.

THE TURKEYS (AROUND 1900)

Many years before, Mother had raised a nice flock of turkeys. She had looked forward to selling them around Thanksgiving. In those days turkeys were bought alive, usually ahead of the holidays, and were killed and dressed by the household, sometimes the same day they were to be cooked; remember, if there was any refrigeration it was a not-too-cold ice box. A Mr. R.H. Hoyt, who had a taxidermist shop at his home, Seven Oaks, on the east side of the county, came to stay a few days at our home in the fall migration and again in the spring to collect birds. On this occasion, Mr. Hoyt had come back late from collecting shorebirds and had roughly skinned them out, covering the flesh sides with arsenic. As it was too dark to finish fleshing them, he would do this the following day. So, in the morning, Mr. Hoyt, after one of Mother's hearty breakfasts, started cleaning up his bird skins and throwing the scraps on the ground. Mother's turkeys began picking up the scraps. In a short time turkeys were falling over, struggling to their feet and falling again. The arsenic killed the whole flock. Many birds collected on the island finally ended up in the Florida State Museum at Gainesville. [Today, Seven Oaks is where the well-known Kapok Tree and restaurant are (McMullen Booth Road), on the east side of Pinellas County.]

THE BOAT THAT WOULD UPSET (AROUND 1905)

When I walked the upper beach one day and found where a washed-in coconut had taken root and become a three-foot palm, I was delighted. From far away shores, more tropical than here, the nuts carried by currents often washed up on the beach. But this was the first that I'd found rooted and growing in a windrow of sea grass. This is the method by which tropic islands get their palms planted by the sea. It was of such little unexpected treats that my life was made. The palm did not survive a frost some time later.

Mail meant much to my father—the local weekly paper, the several magazines he subscribed to and often a letter from overseas. So, on this morning, Father asked me to go to Dunedin after the mail.

This had always meant rowing my small skiff. But on this morning he said, "You can take the *Dinky* if you wish." Now the *Dinky* was a small round-bottomed boat with sail. It had no keel or center board and was tricky to sail, as it seemed to like being upside down rather than right side up. I had sailed it around the bayou and nearby waters often, but had never gone to town alone in it.

The wind out of the east was strong and I had to tack against it. All went well until I neared the mainland shore; then the wind started coming in puffs and I sailed with a lee tiller a great part of the time. I'd just come about from the last tack when an extra strong gust hit. The sail filled, the boat heeled over, but without headway did not answer the rudder and over it went. I climbed out on the high side, a little stunned from this unexpected dunking. Now I thought, if I had had the presence of mind to have let the sheet line loose, just maybe this wouldn't have happened.

A winter visitor (tourist) to Dunedin, a Dr. Badeau, had been sailing not far from my mishap and he came alongside and asked me what I wanted to do. "I want to go home," was all I could say. So the good man said, "That's where we will go." I climbed aboard his boat and we were headed for the island. As we approached the dock, I could see my father standing there. He had sensed something amiss on seeing the doctor's boat coming into the bayou. Father was told of my accident. So he picked up a pail for bailing and he and the doctor sailed off. As soon as we had landed, I headed for the house, not having the courtesy to thank the good doctor. I was wet, scared, and very much embarrassed over my mishap. Dry clothes, and I felt a little better. In a couple of hours, here came Father sailing back in the *Dinky*. My father was always fair and just but stood for no mistakes or foolishness, so I felt I was to at least get a lecture. But he came into the house with a cheerful look. He had done what I was sent to do, gotten the mail. There was even my beloved *Youth's Companion*, a teenager's magazine and what was rare for me, a letter from a former school friend that now lived in another state. If I thought a scolding was coming, I didn't get it. That evening I made what favorite food Father always enjoyed and the day ended on a happy note. As much as I've been on and around the water, this, as far as I can recall, was my only disaster. Like with a horse, I learned the way of the little, cranky *Dinky* and made many safe trips across the sound over the following years.

THE VILLAGE BLACKSMITH

In bygone days, a blacksmith was as necessary to a community as filling stations are in this age. A blacksmith had moved into Clearwater who met all the requirements of Longfellow's poem. He was a large, strong-built man in his middle years, very gentle and soft-spoken. The village people took him to heart. He had time to make small repairs at no charge, loved kids, and fixed bicycles and toy wagons for youngsters as if it was a pleasure, always with a friendly word and pat on the head. When he was asked by a small child, "Mister, can you fix this?" no child was turned away with a curt word. Out of a scrap of metal he could shape useful household articles. For us island people he made oyster knives out of worn-out files. As time went on, the whole town knew him. Women vied for the privilege of having him at their homes for Sunday dinner. He always attended church, coming in with hat clutched to his chest, hair slicked back with water, uncomfortable in a coat. He was included in all the gatherings of the town men. A big thing in those days was to go to Hog Island (now Caladesi) for a coon hunt. The coons were served barbecued at one of the homes and it was strictly a "men's" thing. So there were few, if any, who didn't know, trust and love the village smithy. His shop was in the northeast section of Clearwater and, besides the repair work, he made grills, window guards and fireplace fixtures, among other things. These he often shipped by express to different outlets.

Around this time a rash of burglaries began to take place, something the town had never suffered before. Coachman's Hardware Store was robbed of tools, Harrison's Dry Goods Store of bolts of cloth. The town did have a marshal who walked the streets by day and had little more to do than break up a fist fight now and again. But he could not be on 24-hour duty, so the men of the town joined in. At meetings, nights were appointed to different groups. They were to walk the streets during night hours, listen and try doors of business places to see that they were locked. One of the most enthusiastic of the group was the smithy, always on hand early and giving extra watch duty. As always in those days, the first suspects would be in what was then called the "colored quarters." Had any new Blacks moved in? The resident Blacks were all well-known and trusted. But time went on and nothing was turned up, yet now and again a break-in took place.

At this time a Joe Aunspaugh ran a bakery in town. Often nights, instead of going back to bed after setting the first raising of the dough and waiting some hours for the next step, he would walk, as a rule, to the waterfront. Here on one of his night trips, he found the fish house collapsing into the water, reported it to the owner who got help and saved a large amount of fish and equipment. One night much later on a midnight stroll, Joe heard hammering in the northeast section of town and wondered who, if anyone, would be doing so at that hour. He followed the sound that finally led him to the smithy's place. Looking in an open window, he saw boxes having lids nailed on them. Spread around on a bench were goods that no blacksmith would have use for. Sadly, Joe turned away; now he knew the thief. He carried the news to several of the store owners who had lost goods. It was decided among them that the smithy would be ordered out of town but given time to settle his business first. It was a hard thing to tell a man the town had loved and trusted. On the day he boarded an outgoing train, many came to see him off and there were few dry eyes among the crowd. This incident took place before the turn of the century and it was a common type of justice handed out in small towns in those early years; no arrest, no court trial, just banishment.

MR. ED—A REAL PERSON

Everyone knew him as Mr. Ed. Not an imposing figure; short and slim, sun-burned, scanty hair the color of straw. But such bright, friendly eyes and always the hint of a smile on his lips. He was the friend of all. Each waking hour seemed to be put in being a helpful friend.

He lived on acreage that contained a small orange grove. His elderly parents lived with him in a modest frame house a mile from town. The grove was the only income of the family, but a large garden and flock of chickens supplied part of the living.

Mr. Ed could not seem to let a day go by without being helpful to his fellow men. He visited the lonely, always with a gift of food. If there was sickness in a home, Mr. Ed made the offer of sitting nights. Did someone need help to plant or harvest a crop? He was happy to help.

Mr. Ed was an expert cast-net fisherman. On the waterfront he had a battered skiff tied up and several times a week he would offer fresh-dressed mullet to any who needed or wanted them. A widow with five school-aged children lived near him. He made repairs to her home when needed and supplied them with all he grew and produced.

This widow was known as the "washerwoman," as she took in laundry and was busy from dawn to dusk at her tiresome job.

Mr. Ed's transportation was a fat, well-kept horse and buggy. On a cold or rainy afternoon he would arrive at the schoolhouse as school let out and pile all the children from the country in his buggy and drop them off at their homes. Many of these little folks lived several miles from the school. Mr. Ed had a standard remark, "I was just passing by." Everyone knew he was aware of the weather and had made a special trip to deliver little folks to their homes. Once a year the circus, Barnum and Bailey, came for a one-night stand in a nearby town. This was the highlight of Mr. Ed's year. School let out at noon on circus day. He would invite all the children that could or would go to be his guests. They would meet for the afternoon performance at the railroad station. He would buy tickets for all the children, then tickets

Myrtle hand feeds a flock of chickens.

to the circus and treats of popcorn and peanuts. A happy, tired bunch of children would return by train to their homes in the late afternoon, with a chorus of, "Thank-you, Mr. Ed," ringing in the air.

The 1920 land boom was on. Mr. Ed's parents had passed away and he was alone. A dream entered his heart. He could sell his acreage of land for a large sum, keeping the house and small grove. To the widow's house he went and, with a lot of throat-clearing and stammering, he asked her if she would marry him, as he felt he now had something to offer. More than happy to accept his offer, she became Mrs. Edward White and now Ed had his heart's desire of a family.

THE DOG THAT LIED

The flock of hens provided us with eggs for home use and a few dozen extra a week that went to the grocery store for barter for the few things we did not store in bulk from the mail order house or produce on the place. So on gathering them one day, I found three smashed shells on the floor in front of the nests. I called Gypsy, the dog, showed her the egg shells and gave her the command to, "Go find them." She sniffed about, went outside, and with nose to ground ran ever-widening circles around the hen house, only to come back and let me know she could find nothing. As this was taking place each day, I went over everything I'd ever heard about egg stealers. A rat would carry the eggs off and no coon would be bold enough to come in daylight hours. So what? If I set a steel trap I would catch the hens. It was common practice to poison eggs by chipping a small piece out, placing poison in the egg and sealing with a spot of tape. Not knowing what was eating

Gypsy after a big meal.

the eggs, I did not like to do anything this drastic. So I'd gather them several times a day and maybe catch the thief at his work.

Gypsy always was near the kitchen entrance and was by my side whether I walked a few steps or miles. On this day I could leave the noon meal cooking and run to gather the eggs. I didn't even notice that Gypsy was not around, but as I opened the chicken-house door, who was lapping up an egg? Of all things, my faithful dog. She fell on her back, feet in the air, a dog's way of saying, "I give up." She was not hit, but told in no uncertain words what a bad dog she was and was given a cold shoulder treatment for a few days. That was the end of the egg-stealing. Also, several times a week she received an egg on her food. This same dog was to save my life some time later from a vicious attack by a young, untrained mule I had tried to ride. I was thrown, and as I lay on the ground stunned, the mule reared up over me to stomp me. The dog flew at the mule's head and caused it to shy to one side and miss hitting my body. A few stolen eggs were a small price to pay.

HARVEST TIME

It always seemed the fall of the year was the busiest. It was in the early fall months that net fishing was at its best, as that was the time of year the mullet started gathering in bunches getting ready to school. In those years there was a closed season that ran from November to January. Father was doing much work with his apiary. It would soon be time to extract the summer's crop of honey and put the bees in their winter quarters. There was a big patch of sweet potatoes to dig and sort; some would be stored for home use, the choice ones sold. Also, it was planting time for the winter garden. As everything was done by hand, it all took time, and I often thought the days not long enough to do all the work that was waiting. But the end of day was welcome, and my tired young muscles were glad after a supper of home products to seek the comfort of my garret bedroom. Morning came fast and the same chores were waiting to be done in the new day, yet it was all pleasant, as the results of past work could be seen. I do not remember ever feeling "put on" by the things I was required to do. It was with pride that I looked on a finished task and often my father would remark that I had done a "good job." I was always satisfied with my lot and had no desire to do otherwise. Grown now to womanhood, I sometimes, while in town, would visit a former school-mate, my age but married. I felt I had much the better life and was free. To me, living on a small town lot held no appeal. As I would be crossing the sound on my way home and the tangy salt air from the near Gulf filled my lungs, I thought, "This is the way I want it to be always."

This group of native sabal palms that grew along the Gulf beach of the homestead property was a beloved landmark that Catherine named "The Seven Sisters." Years later, the trees were washed away due to beach erosion.

Myrtle as a young woman.

THE TURNING POINT

It was 1914 and war clouds were hanging over Europe. To me it all sounded very far away. Of course I had read in my history school books of wars. My father was alarmed and was anxious to get the news. He spoke much about how devastating and far-flung this war might become. My small world was around me in peace and I thought it would always be that way.

As Christmas week approached, Father wanted to kill and dress out one of the several corn-fattened pigs we had penned, only waiting for a cold spell to come on. At last there was a brisk northwester with a cold morning. Father had called me early to help with the butchering. The pig was to be shot and bled, then scalded and scraped of hair, drawn, washed and hung overnight. Gypsy would be set to watch near the hung carcass to see that it was not molested by any hungry wildlife. The following morning the cutting up of the meat took place. As Father cut hams and loins he mentioned who would get them for a gift. I said, "Looks like all we will have is scraps." My father paused, and looking at me very seriously, said, "Well, Myrtle, some people don't even have scraps." It was a lesson I didn't forget.

Christmas day came up. We had our usual cedar Christmas tree with its homemade beeswax candles. This year I had a little money of my own making from the sale of frying chickens, and I was so proud that under the tree, gaily-wrapped, was a package for Father, a nice shirt and tie. We were having dinner at home and had invited no guests. So, I was not surprised when near dinner time I saw Father coming up from the dock with two young men. He introduced me to them and said they had sailed into the bayou, that they were on a cruise in a boat they had juſt finished building. He had asked them if they wouldn't like to have Chriſtmas dinner with us and they had readily consented. I didn't know it then, but before a year had passed one of these men was to become my husband. We had a pleasant meal together and learned both young fellows were from New Jersey, were in Florida looking for work and adventure, had built a small cabin sailboat and were going to explore the coaſt, their final deſtination being Miami.

After dinner Father took them over his acreage, as he loved to do with all visitors. The young men were often at our house on weekends for as long as they remained in the section. Then they sent cards from the towns they ſtopped over in on their cruise around the coaſt to Miami. On reaching Miami, the older of the two young men, John

Herman in the Harp Tree, February 1918.

Nevin, bought out the share of the boat owned by the younger man, Herman Betz. John proceeded on the cruise alone, going the length of the Eaſt coaſt, while Herman sought work at his trade as a carpenter. Miami, always a growing city, offered plenty of jobs. Herman and I exchanged letters over the months, and to my surprise he offered marriage. I hardly knew how to take this. All I knew about being married was from the few years I'd seen my mother and father together. I'd noticed how thoughtful they seemed of each other and their companionship; to me that was what marriage meant. I had no woman friend that was close enough for me to talk to. After all, didn't people get married, I thought; wasn't that the way of life? So, after so long a time, I wrote a letter that said yes. If any marriage was ever meant to go on the rocks this one surely was, but the marriage lasted for 55 years "until death do you part." An innocent girl; an ignorant man; the difference between us was like day and night. But at the time none of these thoughts occurred to me.

THE MARRIAGE · SEPTEMBER 29, 1915

The first my father knew of this was when Herman wrote him asking for my hand, a very common practice in those days, as girls did not marry without the consent of a parent. I'm sure my father had mixed feelings but wanted to see me happy. Having been out in the world, he might have thought I should know more than just the island life I loved and was satisfied with. So, in the fall (September),

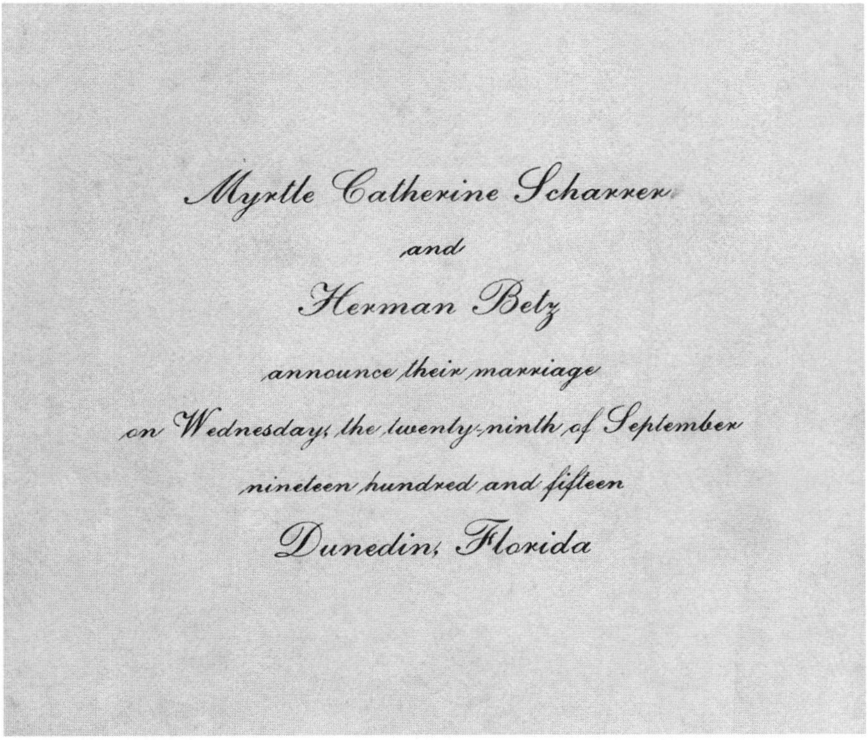

Myrtle Catherine Scharrer

and

Herman Betz

announce their marriage

on Wednesday, the twenty-ninth, of September

nineteen hundred and fifteen

Dunedin, Florida

Announcement for the wedding of Myrtle Scharrer and Herman Betz, held in Dunedin on September 29, 1915.

Herman came to Clearwater, where we met him. He spent the night at our home; next morning we went to Dunedin and were married in the Presbyterian Manse, residence of the minister, by Reverend Wilkie. Mrs. Wilkie, a girlfriend, and my father were the only attendants; no flowers, no music, just the wedding vows. I was married in a grey-blue corduroy dress with a lace vest and high-laced black shoes; Herman in a blue serge suit. We caught a train going to Clearwater and transferred to one going to Tampa, where Herman had rented a room in a boarding house. Here we waited for the steamer that was to take us to Key West. The steamer, the *Sabine,* was a day overdue, having been held up in New Orleans due to a tropical storm in the Gulf. This steamer made the run from New York City to New Orleans, stopping at Savannah, Key West, Tampa and New Orleans. I had friends in Tampa; the husband was in the real estate business, had an office in town, so we visited him there and he took us to his home on some acreage outside of the city. His wife treated us to a nice meal. These people were Dick and May Whitfield. There was a small daughter named Mary. As soon as the steamer docked, we were allowed to go aboard and claim our state room. This was in the evening, and during the early morning hours the *Sabine* took off for the run to Key West.

THE SEA TRIP

What a delight this ship trip was to me. I was right in my element. Flying fish took off in all directions. Bottle-nosed dolphins played about the ship's bow and sea birds followed in its wake. The sea was calm and the day's run very pleasant. We couldn't afford a deck chair, as they cost $1.50 to rent, but strolling the deck from bow to stern was pure joy. The meals were good; I sat at the Captain's right. He was old, fat and grumpy, and his answers to remarks made to him were gruff grunts. That night the cabin was too hot for sleep, as we were in a following wind and had no wind scoop at the portholes. Next morning at dawn we arrived in Key West and took the Overseas Railroad to Miami. The railroad was destroyed by a hurricane in 1935 and never rebuilt. Now there is a good road where once the trains traveled.

A NEW WORLD

On arriving at the station in Miami, Herman hired a horse-drawn cab to take us to the new home, which was a mile-and-a-half west of the city. The fare was $1.50, and here I learned something I was to hear all my married life, either, "It's too high," or "Don't buy any more of it."

The newlyweds in Miami.

Herman had written that he had built us a house. When I saw it, it was rather a shock, a one-room, 14 by 16 feet. Furnishings were a double bed, two straight chairs, a two-burner kerosene oil stove in one corner with two shelves above it, dishes and flatware for two and a frying pan and two small cooking pots. When I was asked what I thought of it, I had to pause and hunt for the right words. Plumbing was a building in the back yard sticking up like a sore thumb. The yard was sand and lime rocks without a blade of grass or a tree. Our neighbors were a widow woman with seven small children on one side and an elderly man and his simple son on the other. This elderly man had a horse and wagon, and five days a week he and his son peddled vegetables, which he bought at a farmers' market.

THE NEWLYWED

So much for my new home and the stranger that was my husband. I hardly knew which way to turn. Everything I cooked had to be bought in town; no more going to the garden or to the bayou for sea food, no more eggs to gather and chickens to dress and cook. It was a new world; Herman was off to his job, if he had one, at an early hour and back late. His wages were $20.00 a week. It was not long

Views of the front and back of the little house that Herman built in Miami. The top photo shows the coral in the front yard. In the bottom snapshot, Myrtle stands in back with pet cats Peggy and Tommy beneath a bare arbor that was covered with vines within a year.

before I found work in a linen supply house, at least that's what the owner called it. Its main business was laundering barbershop towels and hair cloths. It was seldom that I was needed for the full week. The hours were from 7:00 A.M. to 5:00 P.M. on workdays, and the job paid the princely sum of 15 cents an hour. But this little extra was a big thing for me, as I could buy a few extras for the table. My budget for groceries from Herman was $3.50 a week. I wasn't used to this, as living with my father the rule was to get what we needed.

There was much in and around Miami that I could enjoy. The new plants, many tropical, were a joy to me, and I soon had the yard planted. Thinking I was really in the tropics, it was shock in my first winter there to find that a heavy frost one night had blackened all the tender plants. But it was a pleasure to see how fast everything recovered and started growing again. Letters to and from my father kept me informed of my home. A sad note was the death of my dog, Gypsy. In my letters to Father I told many small, white lies. Everything was fine. I spoke of the pleasure I was having improving my new home. I soon learned Herman was a man that set a pattern and went by it

Herman and Myrtle in Miami.

week in, week out. For one thing, every Saturday evening had to be spent at the silent movies, often called the "flickers" in those days. Most likely the movie would be Charlie Chaplin. As I didn't then and don't now care for slapstick, I found it very boring.

But I learned to hold my tongue and keep my thoughts to myself. And my thoughts often, as I sat in the dark movie house, were of home. If I were home, I would be sitting, most likely, on a sand dune above the beach watching the sun pull below the horizon. Flocks of homing birds would be coming in to spend the night on the barrier reef. Then the brilliant western sky would light up in all colors, soon to have the grey shade of night pulled over it all. Leaving the beach I would walk back to the house. The small night creatures would be coming out, and now and then I'd hear a hasty retreat back to the bushes. A nighthawk would zoom overhead and a chuck-will's-widow would call from a tall pine. So the silent movies were just that to me.

THE BOAT

Sometime in our second year in Miami, Herman began building a boat in the back of the lot. He said we would make a trip back to my island home when it was finished. The boat was twenty-eight feet long with a small cabin and powered with a motor and sails. In the late summer the boat was finished, hauled to the Miami River by a hired horse and launched. It was a trim little craft, named *Roamer* after the boat Herman had sold. By this time we had acquired a part Airedale dog and two cats. So the animals were part of the boat's crew and, oddly enough, adjusted to living on shipboard. My father was delighted when he heard we had a boat and planned to visit him. The trip was very pleasant. We caught fish, combed the Gulf beaches and visited the small coast towns, where we would pick up a supply of groceries and fill the fresh water cask. At Cape Sable we collected coconuts. Here on the Cape, in a grove of palms, is the grave of the first Audubon warden, murdered by plume hunters. His headstone gives his name, Guy Bradley. His murder did much to save the egrets, the plume birds, as it brought attention to their plight. This period was likely the lowest in bird life, as they had been slaughtered almost to extinction. Now, thanks to men like Guy Bradley, they are protected and clouds of birds are again to be seen where once there were few.

The place where *Roamer* was launched in the Miami River on July 28, 1917.

Frying fish for breakfast at Blind Pass, Florida. The *Roamer* is in the background.

HOME AGAIN

The trip to the island from Miami was without any unusual events, as we had good weather the whole trip. We used the sails, only using the motor on entering a harbor. In good time, we arrived at the island. Father seemed happy to see us and we were filled in with all that had taken place in our absence. Everything looked familiar, and I took over the cooking on that friendly, old wood stove I had missed so much. I think that pleased my father, as "batching," he had not made the many things he was fond of. But after a few weeks, money running low, Herman said we would go to St. Petersburg where he could get work. We promised to visit Father once in a while, and he seemed pleased we would not be so far away.

FRIENDS

At first we lived on the boat, anchored in the St. Petersburg yacht basin. Then we rented a small house in the north part of town and close to what is now Bayou Placid where we kept the *Roamer* anchored. It was while living here that we became friends with the family of the beacon tender. This was a Mr. and Mrs. Woodward and their daughter, Iva. Mr. Woodward had been lighthouse tender at Egmont Light but, on their daughter's reaching school age, had transferred to take

The home on Coffee Pot Bayou, St. Petersburg.

care of the many beacons marking the ship channel into Tampa. This friendship was to last a lifetime and was one of the closest we ever had. Our interests being much the same, we enjoyed many happy hours together. They were often weekend visitors after we moved back to the island.

It was in the early fall of 1918 that word reached us that a small but very severe tropical windstorm had hit upper Pinellas County and that there had been three children drowned on Caladesi Island. I became much alarmed over my father. It was still war time and the Coast Guard would not allow us to use our boat. So we borrowed a large rowing skiff from the Woodwards, took some supplies and started rowing. The coast chart shows the distance to be about 40 miles. With a head wind and choppy seas, we made Blind Pass the first day in the afternoon. Here we camped on the beach and early the next morning made a fresh start. By the time we reached near Indian Rocks, we started to see the wind damage. Pines on the mainland side were snapped off and the few houses at Indian Rocks at that time on the beach had damaged roofs. Arriving at Father's in the late afternoon, we found him safe. He said one gust of wind had lifted the house off its footings and slammed it back down with a bang. He was a little disturbed over the fact that the morning after the storm, four men came walking down the woods road but on seeing him turned around and walked off. He felt they might have had the courtesy of at least speaking to him.

Herman and Henry with Edward and Annie Woodward at Caladesi in 1923.

THE DEATH-DEALING STORM

That day we walked up the beach to the north end of the island. The children that had been drowned were the Al Garrisons'. Years later, Mrs. Garrison told me that they had come to Caladesi to escape the Spanish flu that was killing so many people at that time. They thought they might avoid it away from others. At the time, a Mr. Haley had a hog ranch on the far north end and Mr. Garrison was to tend it. Mrs. Garrison made the remark that they camped on the island to escape the flu but suffered something far worse.

We spent a few days with Father then rowed back to St. Petersburg, much relieved to know he was all right.

A MEANINGFUL VISIT

Shortly after World War I had ended in 1918, Father made a trip to visit us in St. Petersburg. We were delighted to have him and realized it was, for him, a big thing to come from Dunedin by train. On this trip, he asked us if we wouldn't move to the island to live. He painted in glowing colors its advantages to Herman. I could see that my father was a lonesome man. He seemed to have aged, in my

[123]

Myrtle with a string of sheephead.

eyes, a great deal. I was all for the move. Back to my old way of living, but would city-raised Herman adapt to this life? We had little more now than we had started with three years before, so I could not see we would be losing anything. Herman sounded agreeable to the move. So some few weeks later we loaded up in the *Roamer* our few possessions and, leaving St. Petersburg early one morning, we arrived at the island in the afternoon. For the time being we would live in the *Roamer,* until we could build a small house.

Henry in the rowboat, his favored mode of transportation. The palm fronds in the stern are to quiet the bump of the lead weights as one is letting out a net.

Henry and Herman in a skiff with Rex.   Myrtle in her garden at Coffee Pot Bayou.

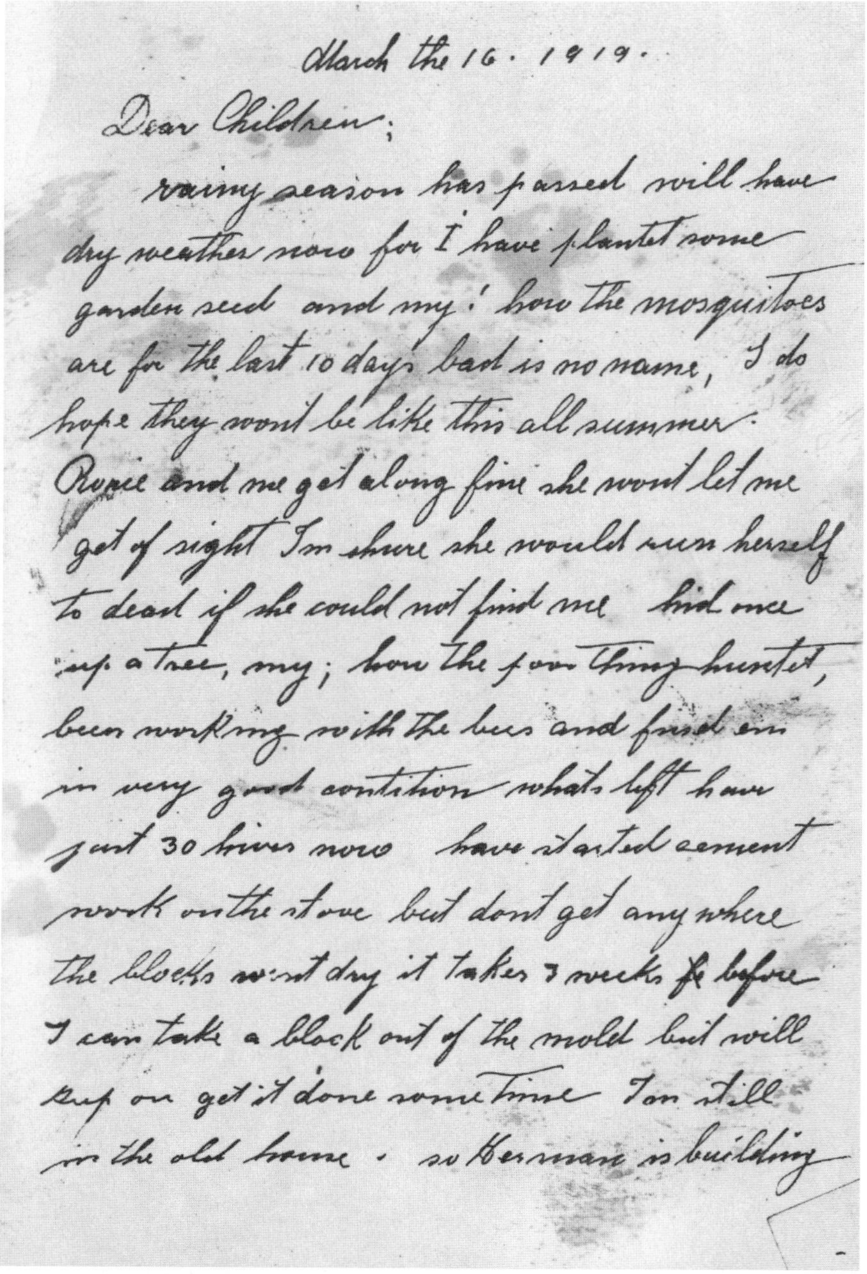

March the 16 · 1919 ·

Dear Children;

raining season has passed will have
dry weather now for I have planted some
garden seed and my; how the mosquitoes
are for the last 10 days bad is no name, I do
hope they wont be like this all summer.
Rosie and me get along fine she wont let me
get of sight I'm shure she would run herself
to dead if she could not find me hid once
up a tree, my; how the poor thing hunted,
been working with the bees and find em
in very good contition whats left have
just 30 hives now have started cement
work on the stove but dont get any where
the blocks wont dry it takes 3 weeks before
I can take a block out of the mold but will
keep on get it done some time I am still
in the old home. so Herman is building

A letter in 1919 from Henry to the "children," Myrtle and Herman, when they were living in Coffee Pot Bayou. He encourages them to move to Caladesi Island: "Myrtle, are you going to clear half of the county for garden and when in good shape give it up [?] better come here and the improvement is your own. Herman and me can go fishing in the gulf."

BACK HOME

Our little house built among the palms was one room with a sleeping porch. I busied myself putting in a garden. Father, with his small needs, had given up gardening. Also, the chickens had, as Father said, been made into soup. So that would be something for the coming spring, chickens to eat and to lay. At this time, out of a blue sky, came a letter from Herman's mother in New Jersey saying she was coming down to spend the winter with us. So with hard-to-spare cash we added a little lean-to bedroom, bought a cot and few furnishings. Mother Betz took an instant dislike to me, the daughter-in-law she had never seen before. I cannot say it was a pleasant winter. I found it rather hard to do all my duties and wait on a guest. Father had at first taken Herman on as a fishing partner, had taught him what he could, then turned over his gear of boats and nets to Herman. With my help, we did very well during the fall months, but when fishing slacked off in the late winter there was a very scanty check from the fish house. I, as usual, had set my traps during the month of January and we got a check from the furs that supplied us with what we called "eating money."

When the winter was over, Mother Betz left for home. Herman, not being acquainted with any of the local contractors, decided to go back to Miami and work at his trade to get a little cash ahead. This would leave me on my own. I made no protest, as I had been in favor of this move. I'd make out somehow, and I did. After some months in Miami, Herman returned. He had sold our little place for $800.00.

Herman's mother, Josephine Betz, standing on the porch of Myrtle and Herman's house on Hog Island, March 1920. By 1928, the home was expanded into the five-room bungalow shown below. The original structure is on the left side, with the expansion to the right.

He set out at once to build a new net boat and buy webbing, corks, leads and line to hang in new nets. My father, who believed in making do with what there was, looked on all this as the foolishness of the "young people," as he called us. Right there and then, I became a fisherman's full-time partner. I'd always helped, but now I took hold at both ends.

NEW FISHING GROUNDS

In the early 1920s, Spanish mackerel were being caught in the Gulf. This called for a larger boat and different type nets. So Herman, who was a first-rate boat-builder, constructed a 28-foot, raised-deck net boat that we could go offshore in. Soon the mackerel fishing shifted to Saint Martin's Reef, called "Big Bank" by the commercial fishermen. This called for a three-hour run from home. The boats of those days only made nine or ten miles an hour on an average. This called for a start from home base at around five o'clock in the afternoon. Herman was captain; it was he who was in the bow looking for the sign of fish. The order "let go" meant to put over the side a drag with a lighted lantern on it; this took the net out. It was run in a circle and, after closing the gap, the boat was run inside the circle to scare the fish into the net. Pulling a deep mesh net out of

Herman with a boatload of mullet weighing about 2,000 pounds.

deep water is hard work and often pulling against a strong wind made it more difficult. But how beautiful were those big mackerel, all silver and gold in color. A night's catch was from a few hundred pounds to thousands. The average price paid in those years was eight cents a pound. After the night's fishing, there was the long, tiresome run to the fish house. Many nights, taking the boat in, cold, wet, tired and sleepy, all I could think of was how wonderful it would be to get into a dry warm bed and go to sleep! But these years of being my husband's fishing partner were the happiest of my married life. There was no bickering between us, no harsh words. Each did his share of the work and it was a most pleasant partnership.

THE HUGE SHARK

In one of our strikes, the propeller picked up the net in crossing. The motor was at once shut down and I went over the stern to clear the prop. This was easy, as I could partly stand on the "iron shoe" that

The Dunedin fish house, located at the west end of Main Street. The dock accommodated vehicular traffic, with a roundabout turn at the pavilion.

supported the rudder. It was a matter of feeling for and freeing the lines and webbing; although it was all underwater work, it was over in a few minutes and I was back in the boat. What made me glance over the starboard side of the boat I don't know, but there, hugged against the hull, was the largest shark I ever saw. His tail fin was at the stern and his huge body, round as a barrel, reached to the bow. I'm sure I'd been in no danger from an attack, as without a doubt he'd had his fill of mackerel picked out of the nets. This monster was seen by many that night, as at the fish house next morning, while unloading, the other fishermen were remarking on his size. I felt like I should tell my story of being overboard with this monster of the deep Gulf.

KING FISHING AND WHERE THE KINGS WENT

In the spring, after the run of mackerel was over, the kingfish appeared. At this time nets were not used, only lures. This fishing was more sport than work. Getting offshore by or before sunrise, we trolled lines with lures at a slow speed. When we ran through a school, there would often be fish hooked on as many lines as were out. These fish ran in weight an average of seven pounds and up. They stayed in the section only a matter of weeks, as the schools came from the south and were traveling north. Sometimes there would be forty or fifty boats in view. This was the time the party boat skippers looked forward to. Many tourists came to the coast just for the king fishing. The real

Myrtle in a 21-foot sea skiff, *The Islander*, built for her by Herman.

sportsmen used rods and reels and played the fish on light tackle. The commercial men used strong hand lines, as their purpose was to catch as many fish as possible. These fish brought the same price at the market as the Spanish mackerel had.

If, during kingfish run, Herman was working in town, I would take my 21-foot sea skiff and be a lone-hander. This was a little before women entered the man's world and as I would pass other boats I would hear this remark shouted over the noise of the motor, "Look there's a *woman* in that boat," and I used to think, "What of it?"

A beautiful sight in the early morning, as the sun was coming up in a clear sky, was to see these great silver fish jump all of eight feet out of the water, and return hardly making a splash.

Party boats often did what was called still-fishing. This was real sport fishing using a rod and reel. The local sardines, the main food of the kings, were chopped or ground up and thrown around the boat (this was called chumming); then the hooks were baited with a live sardine.

In later years, deep nets were used by some commercial fishermen. The schools were spotted by plane and the boats directed to the spot. Catches of fifteen to twenty thousand pounds were made this way. It was a case of killing the goose that laid the golden egg. It was one of the many greedy blunders that have been allowed. The gain for a few, the loss to many.

PROHIBITION

Prohibition (the Volstead Act) was around at this time; it was wise to see little, hear little and say nothing. The lure of quick, easy money turned many a good man into a bootlegger and a lawbreaker. The waterways were the traffic lanes, the Gulf the supplier. On a bar at Big Pass entrance a large sign was erected, "HURRAH FOR THE 12 MILE LIMIT." It did not remain very long; either the sea took it down or someone found it and, out of good taste, removed it. Large ships with cargoes of liquor lay offshore, and those inclined had only to run the 12 miles to obtain as much as they cared to try to land. A schooner, low in the water, was seen anchored in the Clearwater channel. It remained there for some time, then was boarded by the sheriff's men. No one was on board, but the cargo of bottles was labeled "Canada Sour Mash Whiskey." As this was part of those past years, I could hardly leave out mention of the period.

Henry between two cabins built in 1919 with help from Herman. The original chalet-style home was torn down and some lumber was reused. The one on the left is the "winter house" with the woodstove and kitchen; on the right is the "summer house," which was cooler. Neither Henry nor the Betz family ever had electricity at the homestead.

THE LAND BOOM

It was in these early years that the Florida land boom was in full swing. Everyone had the fever. My generous father lent Herman money to invest. He said that if Herman would pay the interest the same as the bank was paying (4%) that he would not expect the principal back. He didn't even want notes, but on this I put my foot down. So we bought some lots in Dunedin and Herman built two small frame houses. But for us it proved to be too little, too late. One house was sold at cost, the other rented; only, because of the Depression coming on, the renters failed to pay rent. Later on, moving to town, we lived in this house. During the Depression years, one lot that had cost $1000 dollars was sold for $50.00. Father never saw any of his money or the interest, and he never mentioned his loss. On his death, I showed the notes to Herman, then burned them. One blessing of the land boom was to make Father comfortable money-wise, as he sold 60 acres of the island property; only one payment was made, but it was enough to see him through without having to do the heavy work that he had been doing. The sale of part of my beloved land made for mixed feelings, and I guess I was happy no development took place. After my father's death, I cleared up the title.

THE HORSE

Father had made me a money gift and it was now that I fulfilled a wish I'd had all my life—to own a horse. This horse was tied into the land boom, as it had been the overseer's horse on a big development. Those were the days that mules and horses were used in land-clearing and hauling material for buildings. This company in the construction business, with headquarters in Georgia, was disposing of what stock

Myrtle with Prince: a horse of her own.

they could, rather than transport them out of the state. So beautiful, bay Prince became my horse. I'd never had jewelry, fine clothes or many other things women long for, but now I had my lifetime longing, a horse of my own. Prince soon learned his way about the island and where the best grazing was. He always came in before dark, where a feed of grain was waiting for him at his stable where he spent the night. What joy it was to ride the beach with my companion. We soon learned to know each other, and Prince was all I ever dreamed a horse could be. He was used also to plow the garden and, hitched to the block and tackle, he hauled out the boats on the ways; work we had done before by hand.

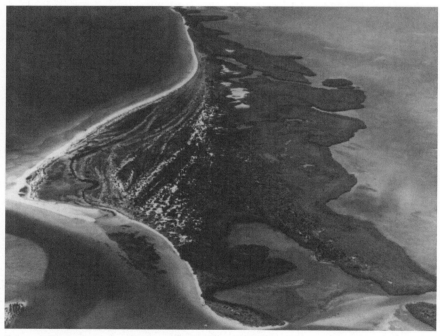

Scharrer Bayou is in the foreground and Scharrer Pass at the bottom right. The narrows, where Hurricane Pass was created by the 1921 storm, is at the top of the photo.

THE WATERSPOUT

One late summer day a waterspout was spotted offshore in the Gulf. It seemed to be headed for the beach. I saddled Prince and rode to the beach to get a better view. A west wind was driving it directly on to the shore. When I was sure it would land, with some urging, Prince and I arrived as it was still about 200 feet from the beach, a foamy wave at its feet. Twelve feet wide and towering to the sky, it swept along. Prince refused to go any closer to the incoming spout, so we stopped about a hundred feet from where it came ashore. There was an odd feeling of being in a vacuum. The spout hit the beach and marched inland, where it ran into a palm tree, twisting the fronds as one might twist a roll of paper, but not uprooting the palm. Shortly after, it seemed to disperse at the foot, and the upper end drew into the low clouds. This was not a solid column of water as they appear to be when seen from a distance, but spray or water droplets. Both Prince and I knew that soon there would be a downpour of rain, so we raced the two miles back to the house. This experience was one of the many that I'll never forget. It was a ringside seat at one of nature's shows.

THE '21 HURRICANE—THE MAKING OF A PASS

In late October of 1921, there was a hurricane that brought a very high tide, the highest in my memory. Early in the morning, after the storm had passed, as usual after a blow, I hurried to the beach. The great wall of water had piled rows of seaweed, lumber, broken small boats and other trash up on the sand dunes. The beach itself was swept clean as if it had been raked. On coming to what was known as the "narrows" or the "haulover," a narrow neck of land that connected the north and south end of the island, I saw a new pass had been cut by the storm. This is now called Hurricane Pass. On this morning it

Henry and the cook house cabin: "still standing" after the 1921 hurricane.

was only about fifty feet wide and very deep where it cut through the land. Erosion has, at this writing 61 years later, made it a main pass to the Gulf.

The name "haulover" might need a little explaining. Those were the days of small, light boats, either sail, oars or poles or all three. So often a roller was carried, the boat pulled up on the shore, roller placed under it and, with plenty of groans and grunts, the boat was pushed over the narrow ſtrait of land from the sound to the Gulf. A line of mangrove was along the sound side and a sparse growth of sea oats on the upland, which was no more than 18 inches above high tide. So this is the ſtory of how the pass was formed and the island became two. By 1941, what had been known and marked as Hog Island was now Caladesi to the south, Honeymoon to the north. The shorelines of Gulf-front beaches changed with each ſtorm, but seldom as draſtically as the cutting of an island in two.

A BABY JOINS US

It was in the fall of 1927, after a visit to my doctor, that I learned we were to have a baby in the spring. I was delighted with the news

Henry adjuſts his battery-operated radio at 4 p.m., time to tune-in news, September 1927.

Herman with baby Marion.　　　　　Myrtle with baby Marion, age 16 days.

and had hopes it would be received by Herman in the same manner. But at the time it seemed to come as a shock to him. Later he became very fond of his child. This did not put a curb on any of my activities. That fall and winter I was still Herman's fishing partner, had a large garden and also had the most successful trapping season ever. As this was the period when every college boy felt the need for a coonskin coat, furs had never been higher in price. So the month's trapping paid my hospital and doctor bills. I felt truly a pioneer woman. In May 1928 a lovely little daughter was born and became a member of the islanders. Maybe at the time I did not realize what a change in my life this event was to be. My commercial fishing days were over.

DEPRESSION YEARS

Now Herman turned his attention to carpenter work in town and the repair and painting of boats. The Depression years were starting and jobs were scarce. These were the bank failure days, and we saw our small savings of over the years go down the drain. It was hard to take, as we had made many sacrifices to build up a little backlog of money in the banks. As always, the good earth provided us with a bountiful table. So all through those hard years we had more than many at that time—plenty of food. Also, we had much to share with some needy families. It meant much to me when a friend said after the Depression was over, "If it had not been for your help, we would have gone to bed hungry many nights." It was big pay to hear those words.

THE LIGHTNING BOLT

Many strange events, some comical, took place; some were unexplainable. Herman came home from a shopping trip to Clearwater. Among his purchases was a casting rod and reel for which he proudly stated he had paid $25.00. Money was very short. Twenty-five dollars was, to us, a large sum. There were many things we needed much more than sporting goods. I'd learned to hold my tongue and never made an issue of anything. After a meal, Herman announced he was going out to try his new fishing tackle. On his return sometime later, I asked him how he liked it and he said he was pleased with the new gear. When I said I would like to use it sometime, I was told very emphatically, "No!" These were the days of cotton casting lines and they had to be dried after use. Herman was stringing the line around bushes, then stepped to a palm tree to hang up the rod and reel. It was a bright sunny day with not a cloud in the sky. As Herman stepped away from the palm, a bolt of lightning hit the tree, splintering the pole into many pieces, and the reel flew in all directions. I went into the house crying. Nothing was ever said about this event, but I did get some hard looks.

A COMPANION

The years rolled by quickly, far too fast. What had been our baby girl was now a sturdy youngster following my footsteps. Trips to the beach were no more alone. Now I had someone interested in bright, pretty shells, someone that asked they all be named. Also, the shorebirds came in for a "What's that?" Now we gathered the "sea mustard" together in the early spring and waded the mud flats in the summer for scallops. If the small child missed the companionship of other children it did not show. Every day seemed filled with some activity that a child could engage in. Before too long, Marion had a little boat of her own and ventured about the bayou with her dog and a fishing pole and spent hours pulling in pin fish. She had a staunch supporter in Grandfather Scharrer. He never returned from town without some

small gift such as a box of crackers or some fruit. I have no memory of his ever giving her candy. He also did some catalog shopping, buying her shoes and dresses which were, as a rule, several sizes too large. But she fast grew into them. Grandpa and Granddaughter spent happy times together visiting. They must have found things of interest to talk about, as the little girl would be all smiles after a chat. My father's dwelling was only a matter of about a hundred feet from our house, so little feet often carried small Marion to his door, and he seemed never to be annoyed by these visits, but would stop whatever he was doing to discuss the events of the day.

Herman with rod and reel and a redfish.

WINDFALL

Work at Herman's trade being scarce during the Depression, he sold a boat we did not need and took a trip to California by bus to visit a brother. This was a drought year, as July had arrived and still no rain. Our cisterns grew low in water, and I was forced to haul water for the house from the mainland. Placing a fifty-gallon barrel in my

Grandpa Scharrer and Marion.

power boat, daughter Marion and I, on an average of once a week, made a run to the Clearwater Fish Company, where they would pass me a hose. In no time we had a full barrel of precious water and were off for home, where it would be used sparingly. Those of the present day who have only a tap to turn on do not appreciate what a supply of water means. Much more precious than food.

On Herman's return home from his trip, he was fortunate to get a boat-building job. Donald Roebling was having a yacht built to cruise in the southern waters. This was a big windfall for us in those tight years. Donald Roebling

Henry liked modern things, such as his airboat. He had one of the first in the area.

was a wealthy young man with an estate on South Clearwater waterfront. His family was well-known, as his grandfather built the Brooklyn Bridge.

THE HEARTBREAK

A fear had entered my heart. Marion was fast reaching school age. I knew Herman had little use for this island living and would be glad for any excuse to get away from it. We had a house in Dunedin left over from the boom time, so were fortunate in that way. The Great Depression was on in full force and the little house had been lived in, but no rent paid for its use. It was in need of cleaning and painting. My worry was my father. He had never complained of any sickness, but I had noticed for some time that he was slowing up. He spent much time in a hammock that was strung in some large oaks by his home. This was not like my father, who had always been busy at something. Could it be old age, and did old age appear so fast?

So in June of 1934, as we made plans for leaving, a heavy knot formed in my chest. How could I walk out on everything I loved? I could see my father was disturbed, but he only said he would not like to see us leave. I put on a brave front and told him we would be coming over to the island often. There was my beloved horse Prince. He would have to learn to get along without his twice-a-day grain feeds; there was good pasture for him. But I did plan on as many trips a week as it was possible to work in. We had several boats we would leave at the island that would need to be looked after, such as bailing them out after rains. They would be sold as soon as buyers could be found. There were many last minute chores to do. Everything I looked at brought tears to my eyes. My mind was in a daze. I knew I must make this move; it was the wish of Herman. I could not be loyal to both my sick father and my husband. No one can serve two masters. It seemed I did not have the right to a choice in the matter.

So here we were in our small frame house in Dunedin, the lot 50 x 100 feet, a two-burner gas plate to cook on. For the first time in many years, I was sleeping in an inside room. I'd slept on an open screened porch on the island.

SMALL DISASTERS

Everything was so different. Marion at once made friends with the neighborhood children, all older than she was. That was fine, only our husky little youngster who had never been sick turned into a lanky, pale child who came down with every known type of cold. Not having been exposed, she had developed no resistance. The first purchase Herman made to turn us into town folks was a car. Within six weeks we were in a wreck, and Marion received a slight concussion. So much for mainland living.

Father knew I liked the Sunday supplement of the *Atlanta Constitution,* a daily newspaper to which Father received a free subscription that came from the editor, who had been an island visitor. So early each week on his trip to town he would walk the mile from the dock to our house to bring it to me. It just broke my heart. This had always been Father's way, to do thoughtful, small things for me. I'd been making as many visits as I could to take him his mail, which had always meant so much to him, and to take small offerings of food that I thought he would enjoy. But there was so little I could do to make up for the loneliness I knew he suffered. I still could not realize that Father was a very sick man; he never had one word of complaint. As the weeks and months passed, I could see him failing very fast and I felt guilty, very guilty, as I felt if we were still on the island he would feel more secure. A very kindly town doctor, Dr. H. E. Winchester, offered to visit Father and see if he could give him any help. Dr. Winchester had his own pleasure boat and after a visit to Father he prescribed medicine. This I saw he was supplied with.

THOSE LAST DAYS

As time went on, I began to make a trip across the sound each evening as early as I could give Herman and Marion the evening meal. Then, with oars on shoulders, I'd hurry to the waterfront where we kept an 18-foot skiff and pull across the sound. It would be dusk when I left; it seemed always the weather favored me. Once it was full moon and such a lovely picture, the orange disk rising and shining

Henry on his dock about 1931.

through the pines that lined the shore, laying down a path of silver on the water. Approaching the island shore, I noticed a change in the air. The west wind funneling into the small pass that led into the bayou seemed so light and heady. There was a point of land I had to round before I could look up to the location of Father's light and it gave my heart a lift to see it shining, as if to show all was well.

I knew Father lit this lamp so I would see it. He was always at the door to greet me and had cheerful questions to ask, as if nothing

Henry's kindness and humor radiate from this late photograph.

was amiss. There was his mail to give him, anything he had asked for on a previous visit, and there was some small amount of cooked food I thought he might relish. He never failed to ask about Marion and often had some small gift for her picked from his trinkets. After I asked if he was in need of anything that I could bring, he would urge me not to linger, as he knew I would have the long row ahead of me. Not once did I ever hear a complaint about his ill health. But there finally came a time when I could see plainly that he was growing so weak that he could barely stand. I spoke to Dr. Winchester and he agreed that Father should not be left alone any longer. Without too much urging, Father consented to come to our home. The last time he was ever on his feet was when he walked into the house from the car that had brought him to our door.

VANDALS AND OTHERS

This was in early December 1934. The daily *Clearwater Sun* got the news and had a write-up on the front page. Father had brought nothing with him and I was very concerned but found it impossible to get over to the island for some days. Fortunately, a next door neighbor was a practical nurse and was willing to stay with Father while I made a trip to the island. My worst fears were justified. Vandals and just plain thieves had made a shambles of the little home. The first thing I noticed missing was Father's violin. Everything had been gone through. Drawers were emptied on the floor; the many keepsakes and trinkets were missing; even the small supply of canned food had been taken. A great fear entered my heart. Suppose Father, by some miracle, became well enough to come back. What would he be coming to? I was going to make sure he was not told of this outrage. I picked up a few discarded things, tried to put some order back, and left. Then as I rowed toward the main shore I tried to think of what all had been removed. Since the beginning, Father had been much interested in radio and had bought each new improvement that came on the market. He had loved to stay up nights and log stations. So the several radios were gone. Among his keepsakes was a silver watch his father had given him while he was yet a small lad. This was a key-winding watch from a time before the stem-winding ones came out. On opening the back, a figure of Christ on the cross filled the space. Jewels of rubies were in Christ's hands and feet. I hope whoever has this watch will value it as much as I would have. On later trips, I found the little house stripped to the walls and then, on a later visit, there were only ashes, as the place had been burned to the ground. A bit of bitterness filled me as there was no sense or reason to it all.

In the early morning hours of December 23, 1934, Father turned his face to the west, as if looking toward his island home, and with only a sigh, went to sleep for the last time.

Now I could never thank him for the many sacrifices he had made for me or all the thoughtful, kind things he had done and the training he had given me. His grey casket, with a spray of red carnations on it, the flowers he loved most, went alongside my mother's. So at last, after 34 years, he was with his beloved Catherine. A way of life had ended forever. A light had gone out for me.

THE END

EPILOGUE

Like a loosely strung necklace, they lie offshore along the coast. They are the front line troops that battle the storm seas. Like front line troops they become weary with the cost of battle and give way.

Their age can be told by the growth they contain. Old islands have stands of pines and hardwoods; new islands, sabal palms and shrubs. A good example of this is Clearwater Beach, which is a very recently built island. Island Estates stands today on the remains of an early island, cut by the sea into five small islands.

As one barrier is being worn down, another is forming outside of it. Caladesi is a very old barrier and is showing its age, witness Hurricane Pass.

In a windy offshore storm look what the beaches are taking, then look at the inland or mainland side where it is so much calmer. That is why the barrier islands are formed: to keep the wear and tear off the mainland shore. This wearing down takes place during each storm. The damage to the outside beach can be severe. Hours of high water and dashing waves will take weeks of work by man to repair. But all the time one island is being worn away, a new line of sandbars is building up offshore to replace it. This does not take place in a matter of years, but over thousands.

Remains of worn out islands can be seen: Anclote Key has Dutchman and North Keys, as an example. Seaside Point is the remains of an early island that has moved to join the main shore.

One of the greatest enemies the few uninhabited islands have is wildfire. Fires destroy the little humus the trees have to live on and they are weakened, so that insects and drought can kill them. Plants of all types are brought to the islands by tides, wind, animals and birds.

Myrtle Scharrer Betz (1987)

Editor's Note: Myrtle was a true lover of the natural world and of wildlife of all kinds. Her narrative describes how she began banding birds for the U.S. Fish and Wildlife Service in about 1920 (page 83). She was a lifetime member of the Audubon Society and wrote articles for the prestigious journal *The Auk*, still published today by the American Ornithologists Union. The following pages reproduce the list of birds she observed during a seventeen-year period, including fifteen years of banding. Her notes and references are included at the end of the list.

BIRDS SEEN ON OR AROUND CALADESI ISLAND
Check List: 1918–1935

1. Common Loon [winter]
2. Horned Grebe [winter]
3. Pied-bill Grebe (Pied-billed Grebe) [winter]
4. White Pelican [April--flocks of 50]
5. Eastern Brown Pelican [resident]
6. Gannet (Northern Gannet) [in Gulf, offshore]
7. Florida Cormorant (Double-crested Cormorant) [nests in pines]
8. Water Turkey (Anhinga)
9. Man-o'-War Bird (Magnificent Frigatebird)
10. Ward's Heron (Great Blue Heron) [nests in pines]
11. American Egret
12. Snowy Egret
13. Reddish Egret
14. Louisiana Egret (Tricolored Heron) [nests in mangrove]
15. Little Blue Heron
16. Eastern Green Heron (Green Heron) [nests in mangrove]
17. Black-crowned Night Heron
18. Yellow-crowned Night Heron
19. American Bittern
20. Eastern Least Bittern (American Bittern)
21. Wood Ibis (Wood Stork)
22. White Ibis
23. Roseate Spoonbill [visitor in August]
24. Lessor Snow Goose (Snow Goose)
25. Common Mallard (Mallard)
26. Baldpate (American Wigeon)
27. Ring-necked Duck
28. Greater Scaup Duck
29. Lesser Scaup Duck
30. Hooded Merganser
31. American Merganser
32. Red-breasted Merganser
33. Turkey Vulture
34. Black Vulture
35. Sharp-shinned Hawk
36. Cooper's Hawk

37. Eastern Red-tailed Hawk (Red-tailed Hawk)
38. Florida Red-shouldered Hawk (Red-shouldered Hawk)
39. Southern Bald Eagle (Bald Eagle) [nests Sept.-May]
40. Marsh Hawk (Northern Harrier)
41. American Osprey [nests]
42. Duck Hawk (Peregrine Falcon) [on daymarkers and beach]
43. Little Sparrow Hawk (Sparrow Hawk)
44. King Rail [nests]
45. Florida Clapper Rail (Clapper Rail) [nests]
46. American Oystercatcher [nests]
47. Piping Plover
48. Semipalmated Plover
49. Wilson's Plover [nests]
50. Killdeer
51. Black-bellied Plover
52. Ruddy Turnstone
53. Wilson's Snipe
54. Hudsonian Curlew (Whimbrel)
55. Spotted Sandpiper
56. Eastern Willet (Willet) [nests]
57. Greater Yellow-legs (Greater Yellowlegs)
58. Lesser Yellow-legs (Lesser Yellowlegs)
59. American Knot (Red Knot)
60. White-rumped Sandpiper
61. Least Sandpiper
62. Red-backed Sandpiper (Dunlin)
63. Eastern Dowitcher (Short-billed Dowitcher)
64. Semipalmated Sandpiper
65. Marbled Godwit
66. Sanderling
67. Black-necked Stilt
68. Herring Gull
69. Ring-billed Gull
70. Laughing Gull [nests]
71. Bonaparte's Gull
72. Forster's Tern
73. Common Tern
74. Roseate Tern
75. Eastern Sooty Tern (Sooty Tern)
76. Least Tern [nests]
77. Royal Tern

78. Cabot's Tern (Sandwich Tern)
79. Caspian Tern
80. Black Tern
81. Black Skimmer [nests]
82. Mourning Dove
83. Ground Dove (Common Ground Dove) [nests]
84. Maynard's Cuckoo (Mangrove Cuckoo)
85. Yellow-billed Cuckoo [nests]
86. Barn Owl
87. Great Horned Owl
88. Burrowing Owl [nests]
89. Chuck-will's Widow [nests]
90. Florida Night Hawk (Common Nighthawk) [nests]
91. Ruby-throated Humming Bird [nests]
92. Eastern Belted Kingfisher
93. Southern Flicker (Northern Flicker)
94. Red-bellied Woodpecker [nests]
95. Red-headed Woodpecker
96. Yellow-bellied Sapsucker
97. Hairy Woodpecker
98. Downy Woodpecker
99. Eastern Kingbird
100. Gray Kingbird [nests]
101. Crested Flycatcher (Great Crested Flycatcher) [nests]
102. Eastern Phoebe
103. Tree Swallow
104. Barn Swallow
105. Florida Blue Jay (Blue Jay) [not resident]
106. Fish Crow
107. Nuthatch (Brown-headed Nuthatch)
108. House Wren
109. Florida Wren (Carolina Wren) [nests]
110. Eastern Mockingbird (Northern Mockingbird) [nests]
111. Catbird (Gray Catbird)
112. Brown Thrasher [nests]
113. Robin (American Robin)
114. Eastern Hermit Thrush (Hermit Thrush)
115. Blue-gray Gnatcatcher
116. Cedar Waxwing
117. Loggerhead Shrike [nests]
118. White-eyed Vireo

119. Yellow-throated Vireo
120. Black-whiskered Vireo [nests]
121. Black and White Warbler
122. Prothonotary Warbler
123. Orange-crowned Warbler
124. Parula Warbler
125. Cape May Warbler
126. Black-throated Blue Warbler
127. Myrtle Warbler (Yellow-rumped Warbler)
128. Cerulean Warbler
129. Blackburnian Warbler
130. Yellow-throated Warbler
131. Black-poll Warbler
132. Florida Prairie Warbler (Prairie Warbler) [nests]
133. Western Palm Warbler (Palm Warbler)
134. Oven Bird
135. Water Thrush (Lousiana Waterthrush)
136. Kentucky Warbler
137. Yellow Throat (Common Yellowthroat)
138. Hooded Warbler
139. American Redstart
140. Meadowlark (Eastern Meadowlark) [not resident]
141. Red-winged Blackbird [nests]
142. Orchard Oriole
143. Baltimore Oriole
144. Scarlet Tanager
145. Summer Tanager
146. Cardinal (Northern Cardinal) [nests]
147. Rose-breasted Grosbeak
148. Blue Grosbeak
149. Indigo Bunting
150. Painted Bunting
151. Goldfinch (American Goldfinch)
152. Red Crossbill [several found dead]
153. White-eyed Towhee (Rufous-sided Towhee) [nests]
154. Seaside Sparrow (Scotts?)
155. Vesper Sparrow
156. Slate-colored Junco [December 7, 1939]
157. Chipping Sparrow
158. Song Sparrow

NOTES

Records compiled during 15 years of banding birds for the Bureau of Biological Survey, now called the U.S. Fish and Wildlife Service. Lifetime member of Audubon Society, wrote articles for *Auk* magazine.

Made field trips with Mrs. Daisy Morrison, Major George D. Robinson, Dr. William Fargo, and Dr. W. S. Blatchley.

References used: *Field Guide to the Birds,* by Roger Tory Peterson; *Florida Bird Life,* by Alexander Sprunt, Jr.

Very few fall records have been noted. Spring migration has been during the month of April, with heaviest flights seen between April 1st and April 24th (land birds). October and March have been the best months for sighting the shore birds.

A TIMELINE

Relating to Caladesi Island, Honeymoon Island, and including significant events in the lives of Henry Scharrer and his daughter, Myrtle Scharrer Betz

by Terry Fortner

This timeline was compiled as an addendum to the 2007 edition of *Yesteryear I Lived In Paradise*. The intention has been: (1) to give an overview of the history of the barrier islands of Caladesi and Honeymoon in the context of Florida's human inhabitants, (2) to recount sequentially some personal as well as historical events that occurred as they relate to the Scharrer and Betz family members, (3) to document the key events that led to Caladesi Island and Honeymoon Island becoming State Parks, and (4) to answer some of the questions that have been frequently asked regarding Myrtle's life.

References include: letters and manuscripts relating to Myrtle Scharrer Betz, transcripts of interviews which Myrtle gave to State Park personnel in 1968 and 1983, numerous articles printed over decades in newspapers (*New York Sun, Clearwater Sun, Tampa Tribune, The Ledger, St. Petersburg Times, The Dunedin Herald,* and *Dunedin Times*), State Park brochures, and texts relating to Pinellas County history. In an attempt to further document the facts as presented here, input from many knowledgeable local residents, historians, and officials was sought. An effort has been made to verify every statement and to keep the account factual.

Timeline

1.806 million (±5,000 years) to 11,550 B.C.E.-Pleistocene Era—Vast sheets of glacial ice, thousands of feet thick, bind up much of the earth's water. The Florida peninsula is nearly twice as wide as it is today.

circa 12,000 B.C.E.—Arrival of first human inhabitants in Florida. Sea level is approximately 200 feet lower than it is at present.

circa 300 C.E.—Glacial melt has slowly returned water to the sea; the shorelines and some of the barrier islands recognizable to present day Floridians are evident. • The earliest native peoples are migratory hunters, traveling in kin-based bands. These communities of people eventually set up permanent settlements around preferred sites for hunting and gathering food. The building of mounds, canals and middens is a reflection of the complexity of these indigenous cultures. Florida is a region rich in aboriginal activity. In ancient times the land area that will be known as "Caladesi" is inhabited by these original Floridians.

1528-April—The Tocobaga people, in the region called "Punta Pinal," experience first contact with the Spanish due to the landing of the Narvaez expedition. • The Tocobaga are a hierarchical society, governed by chieftains, with trade networks that connect to the Mississippi region and Ohio Valley. Contact between Europeans and aboriginal Floridians sets into motion a precipitous decline of the Native-American population due to slave raiding, warfare, and epidemics of disease.

circa 1700s—Ancestors of the Seminole and Miccosukee people are moving into the Florida territory, having been forced out of South Carolina, Georgia and Alabama. Cuban fishermen set up fish camps along the Gulf coast and on barrier islands; one group of Miccosukee joins with Spanish fishermen in the Tampa Bay area and become known as the "Spanish Indians." • African-Americans also live and work in the fish camps, some fugitive slaves, others free migrants from Cuba and other Caribbean locales. Besides salt-fish and smoked seafood, the "catch" includes honey, plumes, hides, tame squirrels, and songbirds to be used as pets. Regular trips are made to transport the items to market in Havana.

circa 1780—One fish camp, or "rancho," of the Tampa Bay region is located on the southern tip of Caladesi. This fish camp is operated by a man called "Caldees;" the island is referenced as "Cayo de Caldees" or "Caldees' Island." • This is one of the stories told to explain how the name for Caladesi originated.

1763-1783—Florida is in English possession for 20 years. The barrier islands off the Pinellas coast continue to be used for fish camps and serve as campgrounds for crew members when smaller craft are sent ashore to make landings. • In 1783, at the end of the American Revolutionary War, Britain returns the Florida territory to Spanish control.

1821—The U.S. acquires the Florida territory from Spain following continuous invasions associated with the War of 1812 and ongoing Native American removal campaigns. • During skirmishes between Spanish and U.S. forces, the fish ranchos are subject to raids and destruction. African-Americans, when captured, are enslaved. "Indians" are forced to inland reservations and assigned an "Indian Agent." Some individuals withdraw to even more remote areas of south Florida.

1834—Hillsborough County is created from an area that was previously part of Alachua and Monroe counties. • During the Second Seminole War (1835-1837) two military outposts are established in the County, Fort Brooke in Tampa and Fort Harrison in Clearwater. The military presence is established with the intention of: 1) overriding any Spanish and Cuban business interests in the region, 2) encouraging settlement by U.S. citizens, 3) capturing escaped slaves, and 4) forcing Native Americans onto reservations. Although there are interludes of cooperative interaction amongst individuals of differing cultural heritage, the general trend is toward empowerment of white settlers and exclusion and expulsion of Black, Spanish, Cuban and Native claims to land ownership. The banishment of the Seminole and Miccosukee people allows for accelerated movement of U. S. settlers into the area; the Armed Occupation Act and other homestead laws give further enticement.

1845—Florida is granted Statehood. Increasing numbers of hardy, self-reliant settlers continue to stake out claims, especially in areas where water access affords a means of transportation and sustenance.

1848-September 25 and October 12—Hillsborough County is decimated by two brutal hurricanes. • The fish camp on Caldee's Island is subsequently abandoned. The effect of the hurricane surge and wind damage is evident on Caladesi and in the entire region well into the 1900s.

1852—Richard L. Garrison records the first land deed in what will become the Dunedin area. • The barrier islands of the Tampa Bay region continue to be visited for purposes of hunting, fishing, and beach picnic outings. There are instances of homesteader activity for brief periods of time on the various islands, but no long-term permanent residence is established. Because there is habitat with forage and a fresh water pond, Caladesi is used as a free-range for raising hogs. The early settlers of the Dunedin and Clearwater area reference the island as "Hog Island."

1858-April 12—Henry Scharrer is born in Waedenswil, a town on Lake Zurich, Switzerland. He attends public schools and graduates from the University of Zurich. • Three separate birth-years for Henry Scharrer are on record. Especially in his later life he tells people that he is older than he actually is, as he enjoys the forthcoming compliments. This attribute of being a storyteller and of embellishing the truth is a recurring theme in the stories that have come down about Henry. He is robust, capable, independent, hard working, humorous, and extroverted.

circa 1880s—Fishermen from Cuba continue to work in the Gulf waters and Caladesi is a stopover for them. A story is told that a Spaniard named "Desi" had once lived on the island bayou ("cala" in Spanish) so this becomes another accepted explanation as to the derivation of the name for Caladesi.

Sea oats and other native plants frame an island vista.

1883—Henry Scharrer arrives in New York City, en route to an assignment to inspect dairy operations at Swiss settlements in Wisconsin. During the next five years he travels and works his way westward, eventually reaching San Francisco.

1887-1888—Peter Demens secures financial partners and extends the construction of the Orange Belt Railway into west Hillsborough County. This train system makes overland travel to the mid-Gulf Coast region of Florida significantly more expeditious and opens the way for freight and passenger service. • Henry Plant buys the railroad in the late 1890s and converts it to standard gauge.

1887—Henry Scharrer arrives in the Gulf Coast section of Florida. He purchases a lot along the Hillsborough River and works in Tampa, helping to construct the Plant Hotel. • In 1931 this hotel becomes the home of the University of Tampa.

1888—Henry "discovers" Caladesi while taking a shakedown cruise in the Gulf of Mexico on his newly refurbished sloop, *Anna*. Upon exploration of the island, Mr. Scharrer is so impressed that he decides to make his home here. • Mr. Scharrer befriends a crew of fishermen from Cuba who visit with him each time they are in the area. Over many years of interaction, gifts and knowledge are exchanged. Henry hears the Spanish name and starts to reference the island by the name "Caladesi," which he translates as meaning "beautiful bayou."

circa 1889—Henry applies to become a United States citizen. He takes a job at a sawmill three-miles east of Dunedin in order to acquire the lumber and materials to build a home on the island. First a small shed is built on site to store materials and to use as a shelter. Next Henry constructs a permanent home and a rain barrel (cistern). • Eventually several shallow wells are dug to use for watering stock but the primary source of water on the island for drinking and home use is from the collected rainwater.

1890—Henry takes up permanent residence on the southern 156 acres of Caladesi (which is still known locally as Hog Island). He plants a garden, establishes an apiary, and raises hogs; also he fishes and captains charter fishing tours for visitors. At the time Henry's homestead is established, the entire island is approximately 1,200 acres in size.

1892-1920—The Scharrer island homestead becomes a regular destination, a type of tourist attraction, especially for winter residents and visitors to Dunedin and Clearwater. People visit by the boatload. Henry demonstrates his beekeeping operation, shows the vegetable garden, and takes the groups on walks to points of interest. A full tour includes a rare double-trunk slash pine tree (called "The Harp Tree"), the small fresh water pond, an oak hammock (Henry calls this "the cathedral"), the Gulf beach, a grouping of sabal palms (given the name "The Seven Sisters" by Catherine McNally), the eagles' nest, Native-American mounds, and the heron rookery. Each island tour concludes with a picnic meal eaten at outdoor tables set up beneath the shade of palms and live oaks at the homestead property.

1894-April 14—Henry Scharrer marries Catherine "Kate" McNally (born in Ireland, October 4, 1864) of Cleveland, Ohio. The wedding is held in the palm grove near Henry's island home. Catherine had traveled to Dunedin as a companion to Mrs. L. H. Malone, whose husband is a yachting enthusiast. Catherine's skill as a cook is an added attraction for homestead visitors. • The Malone family and their guests often visit with the Scharrers; many photos document the frequency of their interaction.

1894-1899—Repeated, severe winter frosts kill back the mangrove along the coastal shoreline and discourage the citrus farmers inland. • Dramatic cold spells, brief in duration but devastating in effect, have punctuated the livelihood of Florida farmers of every generation.

1895-February 22-3:00 p.m.—Myrtle Catherine Scharrer is born at the island home during a dramatic freeze and winter storm which for three days prevents tidal water from flowing into the Bay, making travel by boat impossible. Henry is stuck on the mainland, having gone to fetch the doctor. A mid-wife had been hired to stay with Catherine. Meanwhile, a couple from Dunedin is stranded on the island and takes shelter at the Scharrer cabin. • In an interview given to the *Clearwater Sun*, published in July of 1950, Mrs. Sarah F. Douglas relates the story of this occurrence. "We rowed across the bay to Scharrer's Island. While we were there a big storm and freeze came up, and blew all the water out of the bay. At practically the same time, Mr. Scharrer, who owned the island, had rowed to Dunedin to get Dr. Badeau, as his wife was about to give birth to a child. We had to stay on the island for three days and he had to stay in Dunedin three days before there was enough water to cross the bay. It was so cold that three women had to sleep in one bed to keep from freezing. Fortunately one of the women was a mid-wife and when Mr. Scharrer returned his child was already born. . . ."

1895-1901—As the child matures, Catherine imparts to her daughter her own interest in botany and shelling, affection for animals, and proficiency in and enjoyment of cooking. Myrtle learns to sew and embroider, as this is a necessary skill, and is expected at the time. • Very early in life Myrtle learns that her father, in order to protect his property from poachers and others who have ill intentions, occasionally must resort to firing a warning shot into the air to drive away trespassers. He has a lookout ladder and welcomes all visitors who come openly as sightseers. He gladly shows visitors over his sanctuary but through the years there are some who cannot be welcomed, or if welcomed, cannot be trusted. On occasions when Henry is out to fish or away to market, Catherine must be prepared to defend the island home.

1897-January 23—Henry receives Homestead Certificate No. 12580, signed by Grover Cleveland, for Application 18720, which grants him title to 156 acres on the southern part of Hog Island, now often referred to by locals as "Scharrer's Island." The island bayou begins to be referenced as "Scharrer's Bayou."

circa 1900—Naturalist R. D. Hoyt, of Seven Oaks, collects bird specimens using the Scharrer homestead as base of operation. This collection is sent to the Florida State Museum in Gainesville. • Seven Oaks was located north of the present day intersection of McMullen Booth Road and Drew Street in Clearwater, Florida. Mr. Hoyt planted the kapok tree that is still an area landmark at the date of this writing, April 2007.

1901—Catherine's health deteriorates; surgery is attempted. Henry's journal records the regular purchase of morphine, indicating that she is in great discomfort.

1902-April 8-1:15 a.m.—Catherine Scharrer, age 38, dies. She is buried at Clearwater Municipal Cemetery, located at the intersection of Myrtle Avenue and Lakeview Road. • This is the first and last funeral that Myrtle will ever attend. When Henry and Myrtle return to the homestead, they find that the kitchen house has been damaged by fire and the home has been ransacked.

circa 1902—Some streets of Clearwater are being named; Myrtle Avenue is named for "that little girl on the island." • This entry is based on anecdote only, as no actual documentation has yet been revealed.

1903—Dr. Clarence B. Moore, an associate of the Philadelphia Academy of Natural Science, excavates a burial mound on Caladesi. He notes that this mound has been "woefully dug into," and that no artifacts were placed with the burials. He is of the opinion that the mound is quite ancient. Dr. Moore removes a total of 19 skulls, 3 for pathology study, and counts 33 skeletons.

1903—Myrtle, eight years old, learns to prepare meals on the wood stove and becomes adept at using tools and fishing gear, handling a rifle, rowing and sailing a boat. Henry digs a canal from the gulf side to the bay side south of the homestead. Myrtle assists in this project as well. The intention is to shorten the trip across St. Joseph Sound to Dunedin. • Today this pass is called "Scharrer Canal." The small island cut off to the south is called "Malone Island."

1904-1908—Myrtle attends school in Dunedin, rowing her skiff daily to and from home. Through Scharrer Canal, it is two miles one-way to the mainland. Whether the trip is pleasant or difficult depends on the weather.

circa 1908—Henry is sometimes away working and young Myrtle is left to tend the homestead. Because of the location of the dock, it is easy for passersby to see that Mr. Scharrer's boat is away. On more than one occasion Myrtle takes refuge in the attic with a locked trap door, her loaded rifle at the ready, as she has been instructed to do. She can overhear as the interlopers walk the property, talk, and even come into the house; she often knows exactly who these people are, as she recognizes their voices. • Myrtle learns that, for some reason, there are always disingenuous people in the world.

1911-1914—The Thomas Zimmerman family moves onto the northernmost 54-acres of the island. After receiving the land grant, they return to mainland living. • The Zimmerman homestead was located on what is now Honeymoon Island State Park.

1912-January 1—Pinellas County is created from what was previously West Hillsborough.

1912-1915—The Emil Goss family builds a home on a 90-acre tract north of the Scharrer homestead. They stay to prove up on their title to the land and then move back to the mainland.

circa 1912—Myrtle works for the Bass family during their winter visit to Clearwater.

Herman waiting for the train to Miami.

1914-1918-(World War I)—Wartime rationing doesn't cause so much hardship to the islanders because they already catch and grow most of their own food, and sail or row to get around.

1915-September 29—Herman Christopher Betz of Newark, N.J. (born Dec. 29, 1887) and Myrtle Catherine Scharrer are married in a ceremony held in Dunedin, Florida. • The newlyweds travel to Miami to live in a home that Herman has built there.

1916—Herman has a construction job helping to build Vizcaya, a Renaissance-style villa, winter residence of industrialist James Deering. Meanwhile, in the yard of the Miami home, he builds a sailboat. It will be named *Roamer II*. Myrtle puts in a south Florida garden and works part-time.

1917—Myrtle and Herman sail the *Roamer* from Miami and experience a glorious and adventurous cruise, fishing and camping along the coastal route. They visit with Henry and decide to move back to Pinellas County from Miami. • First they live aboard the *Roamer* in St. Petersburg harbor; then for a time they live in a house at Coffee Pot Bayou as Herman continues construction jobs.

1918-September 18—Three young children of Al and Estelle Garrison are tragically drowned at "the narrows" on Hog Island during a small but locally severe hurricane. Henry weathers the storm at his island homestead,

Herman doing a handstand.

Myrtle in 1925.

A group of visitors relax under Henry's watchful eye.

where no lasting damage is done. • Wartime restrictions will not allow the use of sail or power boats, so Myrtle and Herman row the 40 miles from St. Petersburg in order to check on Henry's welfare.

1919—Myrtle and Herman return, invited by Henry, to build a home and live on Caladesi. Myrtle sets to work gardening and trapping. Herman pursues boat building and repair from a shop on the island. On occasion Herman travels away from home to work at construction. From Miami, Herman sends a gift to Myrtle—six seedling Australian Pines to plant. • Lumber from the original homestead home is reused by Herman in the building of two cabins for Henry's use, one is a "winter" home—kitchen with wood stove and fireplace, the second is a "summer" home with screened windows and door for ventilation and cooling comfort.

1919-1934—Myrtle bands birds for the Bureau of Biological Survey. • This later becomes the U.S. Fish and Wildlife Service.

1920—Myrtle actively seeks to learn more regarding the animals and plants that are found on the island. She hungers for scientific information and accumulates reference books that help her to identify birds, shells and plants. She begins a bird list that is kept for fifteen years and documents all bird species seen on and around Caladesi Island.

1920-1928—Myrtle and Herman operate a commercial fishing venture.

1920-1934—Myrtle traps raccoons every winter; this task is not undertaken for pleasure but as a way to bring in extra income.

1920—Woman's Suffrage is enacted in the United States. Myrtle, along with many other women, can now exercise a right to vote. • In 1916 Clearwater held a successful special election to adopt a new city charter, one of the features being municipal suffrage for women. The women of Clearwater had their first opportunity to vote on October 23, 1916, for a $10,000 bond issue to aid in building a two mile bridge across Clearwater Bay to the "Island on the Gulf," (a.k.a, "Island Park," Shell Island," and "Picnic Island.")

1920-1933—Prohibition is enacted and "rum runners" lie at the 12- mile limit offshore. As Myrtle writes in *Yesteryear,* for the island family, "it was wise to see little, hear little and say nothing."

1920-1934—Henry's fame as an entertaining host and knowledgeable observer and protector of his island kingdom continues to draw visitors. He is the subject of newspaper and magazine articles.

1920-November—An article by A.E. Ibershoff in *Field and Stream* magazine relates a visit to Mr. Scharrer, "We followed him into the palmetto jungle over well-trodden paths and were soon astounded at his phenomenal familiarity with every detail of the tropical flora...." Mr. Scharrer is quoted in dialect to portray his Swiss-German accent and several of his "tall tales" are retold. The article gives a little description of the inside of his winter cabin, "...which was neatness itself. His stove was made of sand and cement three stories high, the uppermost being the fire pot, below it the oven for baking and roasting and the bottom space for drying his fuel. On the walls were numerous nautical instruments, barometers, hygrometers and thermometers, and with great solicitude he produced an old violin, and, holding it so we could see the inscription on the inside, we read: 'Stradivarius 1763.'" • Fritz Kreisler played this instrument when he visited with Mr. Scharrer. This violin is among the items stolen at the time of Mr. Scharrer's death.

1921-October 25—The most severe hurricane since 1848 moves across Pinellas County. Hurricane Pass is created at the part of the island which is referred to as "the narrows." Myrtle is the first person to view the newly formed pass on the early morning following the storm, as it is her delight to walk the beach after any big blow. The Scharrer and Betz homes are briefly flooded, but no permanent harm is done. • The separated islands are referenced now as Hog Island and Scharrer's Island.

1921-1925—Known as the "boom" time, Florida real estate is the source of fortunes made and lost. Henry, badgered by land speculators, accepts a $15,000.00 down payment on 59-acres of his land, but the deal falls through, as Henry has predicted it would.

1928-February 1—The name "Hog Island" is officially changed to "Caladesi Island" (United States Board on Geographic Names). This name change is proposed by the Dunedin Chamber of Commerce on December 30, 1926. The name "Caladesi" had been kept alive in oral tradition and was the place name preferred by Mr. Scharrer who makes no objection to the name Hog Island but thinks that Caladesi is a name more appropriate to the beauty of the island.

1928-May 8-4:18 p.m.—Marion Ann Betz is born at Morton Plant Hospital; she and Myrtle remain there for two weeks, under doctor's orders,

Marion with Polly, circa 1930.   Herman among sabal palms on the island.

while Myrtle recuperates. Marion's first exciting life event is a boat trip home to Caladesi.

1929—The infamous year of a "crash," followed by years of nationwide economic depression. Mr. Scharrer is one of several deposit-holders responsible for supporting the Bank of Dunedin, one of the few local banks that does not fail.

1929—A local developer sells all his materials including his cavalry horse, "Prince." Prince is brought to Caladesi and becomes a special companion and pet; Myrtle enjoys many rides along the beach. Prince willingly works in harness to plow the garden and to pull boats up the ways. He earns his keep both as a work and pleasure horse.

1930-April—Robert H. Davis writes a four-installment article for the *New York Sun* with a Robinson Crusoe theme. The article flamboyantly relates a tale of Henry's early years on Caladesi, his marriage to Catherine and her passing. Mr. Davis especially recounts Henry's fascination with and protection of the native birds. Mention is made of Myrtle: "Under my hand and eye our daughter was brought up here on this island. I made a strong and self-reliant woman of her—a hunter, a sailor . . . I taught her to love nature."

1930—A young Double Yellow-headed Amazon parrot (*Amazona oratrix*) is given to Mr. Scharrer as a gift by his Cuban fishermen friends. This parrot, "Polly," becomes Marion's special pet and picks up many words and phrases: i.e. chanting ABC's, calling "Marion" in Myrtle's voice, questioning "Any mail today?" in Mr. Scharrer's voice, and, predictably, enunciating "Polly wants a cracker." Once acclimated, Polly is often allowed to be free during daytime hours; she remains in the vicinity of the homestead, liking most of all to climb around in the oak trees. Polly lives until 1970.

1931—Dr. W. S. Blatchley writes of Mr. Scharrer in *My Nature Nook,* "[H]e is a man of intelligence and interested in all that pertains to the out-of-doors, I am always glad to visit him at his island home and hear him tell of the many interesting objects found thereabouts. For years he made his living as a fisherman but now keeps bees, having 71 stands which make honey throughout the year."

1931—Myrtle writes vignettes detailing aspects of her observations of island life called *Things Seen and Heard but Not Seen: An Islander's Twelve Months.*

Henry polishing his rifle.

Myrtle taking aim with her rifle.

1932—Myrtle keeps a diary and calls it *An Islander's Year*. An article she submits is accepted for publication in *Motor Boat Magazine*.

circa 1932—Mosquito ditches are dug on the barrier islands by county decree. At Caladesi the ditches cut through the burial mound on the bayside of the island. This project includes dynamite being set off to "deepen" the fresh water pond. In an effort to save something, Myrtle and Marion collect mud turtles from the island pond and keep them in an outdoor fish pool beside the Betz house, returning them to the pond area a week or so later. According to Myrtle, the pond did not regain its former health and beauty. • Mosquito control was a fervent issue for Florida, residents demanded relief from biting insects and it had been determined that disease could be transmitted by mosquitoes. As with other undertakings of public works programs, although the intention was to serve the public good and to enhance the prospects for increased development and economic expansion, some of the consequences were unfortunate.

1933-November 17—While he is burning trash, the fire escapes Henry's tending and burns the woods north of the homestead. Friends from Dunedin and Clearwater rush over by boat to help protect the homes, outbuildings, and the Harp Tree. • Henry regularly fought fires on the island. Myrtle later feels the shock of this incident hastened Henry's death.

1934-June—Myrtle, Herman and Marion move from the island to Dunedin, in order that six-year old Marion can become adjusted before she enters school in the Fall. They reside at 515 Locklie Street, in a home built by Herman during the boom time.

1934-December 23-3:00 a.m.—Henry Scharrer, "King of Caladesi," dies. He is laid to rest beside his beloved Catherine at the Clearwater Municipal

The final resting place of Henry and his beloved Catherine.

Cemetery. Herman attends the funeral as the family representative. • It is during the laſt weeks of December 1934, while he is being cared for by Myrtle in Dunedin, that Henry's island home is robbed of personal items.

1935—Living on the mainland, Herman is pleased to purchase an automobile, a Plymouth. He ſtarts to travel every summer to conſtruction work in North Carolina, and later, New Mexico. Myrtle acquires King, another horse, as Prince has been allowed to remain at Caladesi. Now she frequently rides in the woods and groves eaſt of Dunedin.

1935—The Florida Park Service is created by the Legislature under the Florida Board of Foreſtry. A budget of $25,000 per year is appropriated for ſtate park purposes.

1935-A caretaker, Mr. Allison Vrooman, lives at the Scharrer homeſtead in an effort to keep the property from being vandalized. Myrtle discusses her willingness to sell her birthplace as a wildlife refuge and camping area for nature lovers. This had been Henry's expressed wish, also. At the time there is little intereſt in such an idea, and Myrtle receives the impression that influential people regard this as a foolish concept. • Allison Vrooman continues to live at the Betz home on Caladesi until approximately 1954.

The beach cabins.

1936—Herman, with assiſtance from Allison, builds three cabins on the outer beach, south of Bird Key. The cabins are designated as "Sea Drift," "Spin Drift," and "Sand Drift." The Betz family uses Sea Drift as their own place to ſtay on island visits. The other cabins are available as gueſthouses for family friends and for rental use.

circa 1937—Dunedin city commissioners approve purchase of 84-acres adjoining Scharrer property. The land is obtained from the Florida State Internal Improvement Board where it had reverted for taxes due, and Dunedin is given firſt option. The price paid is $12 an acre. Civic leaders talk of using part of the land as a summer camp for Dunedin boys and girls. • At this time, there is talk of building a causeway to Caladesi. This possibility was wrangled over and discussed well into the 1960s.

74—Honeymoon Isle in the Gulf of Mexico

A vintage postcard view of Honeymoon Island.

1938—Dredging equipment is brought to the north end of Honeymoon Island and focused excavation work takes place. Local people are warned away by rifle shots when they seek to investigate. The operation is discontinued quite abruptly. A lasting mystery is created as to who was directing the work, what was being sought, and what may have been found. • Stories of buried pirate treasure are told and persist to this day.

1938—Clinton Washburn, New York investment broker, purchases North Hog Island for $25,000.00 and embarks on an ambitious marketing scheme. By 1941 an airstrip, dock, dining hall, "The Kings Palace" clubhouse, and forty thatched cabins are constructed. Drawings for free honeymoon vacations to newly-wed couples are advertised nationally in magazines and newsreels. The honeymoon concept is a publicity bonanza for the local area. The name of Honeymoon Island is proposed and wedded to North Hog Island, for better or for worse. (This is not a comment on the suitability of the name, only a reference to marital vows!) Much attention is given to the venture, and the facility becomes a destination for local outings and meetings as well as drawing people from out of state. The heyday of the honeymoon cottage vacations is abruptly ended by Pearl Harbor.

1939—Herman and Marion Ann attend the World's Fair held in Flushing Meadows, New York. During this trip they visit with Herman's relatives in Maplewood, New Jersey.

circa 1940s—Intra-coastal waterway channels are dredged, leaving spoil islands alongside. This dredging work makes boat travel more efficient and less hazardous, but, according to Myrtle and others who make their living from fishing, it has a deleterious impact on the health of St. Joseph Sound. Sea grasses, which grow on the mud flats and are a valuable and necessary part of the marine environment, are smothered by the silt. This leads to loss of habitat and a decrease in shellfish and fish in the areas close to shore. Other factors are also at work, such as disregard for catch limits and refusal by commercial and sport fisherman alike to observe a seasonal allowance for the fish to spawn so that populations can be replenished. Meanwhile, development policies allow raw or partially treated sewage and storm waters to run directly into the Gulf. By the 1950's the "clear water" is no longer clear. • Eventually legislation is enacted that seeks to remedy the pollution caused by storm water and sewage run off. These efforts are still ongoing, by necessity, as pollution is a continuing aspect of intensive development. Increasing public awareness about the problems of run-off and fisheries habitat losses are providing incentives to address this serious problem.

Herman seated outside the SeaDrift cabin on the outer beach.

1942-1945—U.S. enters WWII; Myrtle takes courses in first aid and home nursing, serves as member of the local Red Cross and as First Aid Chairman for the local Civilian Defense organization. She is active in other war support efforts, as was almost everyone during those years. Myrtle takes a job at the Dunedin Fish Company, managing the market, which often involves cleaning thousands of pounds of fish under deadline to be shipped out by train. During the war, Herman works at the shipyards in Tampa. The barrier island beaches are used for military training maneuvers; Donald Roebling's amphibious Alligator Tank is tested, and pilots use the beaches for strafing exercises.

[173]

circa 1943—Joe and Wilmer James are regular visitors to the island cabins with their mother Frances, who is a good friend of Myrtle's. The boys enjoy watching the military exercises. One day, while Myrtle walks the beach and the children are playing, a single engine airplane with one pilot goes down in Big Pass. Myrtle rows out to the downed plane, brings the body of the pilot on board and stays with the plane until the authorities arrive. • This eye-witness account was related by Wilmer James.

1944-1945—Myrtle writes a weekly article called "Pinch Hitting for the Old Salt" for the *Dunedin Times*. The "Old Salt" is the regular columnist who is away serving in the military. The column relates news of the fishermen, practical wisdom, dock-side gossip and seafood recipes. Myrtle reports anonymously, which gives her the advantage of overhearing lots of "material."

1946-July 10—Myrtle Betz sells 157-acres on Caladesi to Francis L. Skinner, Dunedin City Commissioner and packing house owner, for $50,000. An updated survey adds one acre to the original homestead. The sale includes the homestead tract with the five-room bungalow, which had been the Betz home, and the three beach cabins. • An anecdotal source says a deed restriction was placed on the sale by Myrtle, regarding the Scharrer home site: it was to remain a wildlife refuge where no alterations would be made without the permission of The Audubon Society and the Clearwater Marine Science Center.

1946-1954—Herman and Myrtle buy a 10-acre fruit ranch in Bent, New Mexico. For eight years they own and operate it. Myrtle spends summers, but only one cold winter there, proclaiming, "This is enough!" At some interval during these years Myrtle and Herman take a road trip that includes a visit to locations in California and a drive along the Oregon coast, where Myrtle especially enjoys the scenic beauty.

1947-1948—Myrtle accepts a job at Honeymoon Island for one season. She resides in one of the thatched cabins and operates the dining hall. She has Polly and a Siamese cat named "Punky" as her companions. Her pies, baked bread and home-

Marion Ann Betz and Gerald Max Thorp.

style cooking are a draw to visitors, and she is introduced to celebrities who are flown in for publicity visits.

1950-December 31—Marion Ann Betz and Gerald Max Thorp of Green Cove Springs, Florida, are married at the First Presbyterian Church of Dunedin.

1953—The Dunedin City Commission makes application to extend city limits to include all of Caladesi and Honeymoon Islands. The island land-owners formulate plans for commercial and residential development of Honeymoon and Caladesi; this includes a proposal to build a causeway to Honeymoon Island. • Public thinking at this time is generally in favor of development of these islands.

1954—Myrtle and Herman Betz retire to 1.3-acres on Sutherland Bayou in Palm Harbor. Herman builds a kitchen house, a shop and a small home. Myrtle once again puts in and maintains a prolific vegetable garden. She raises mallard ducks and bobwhite quail. Herman engages in his first-rate talent for carpentry and son-in-law Gerald is inspired to build benches and tables, also. Three grandchildren, David (1951), Terry (1953) and Suzy (1955), are regularly dropped off for vacation and summer visits.

circa 1956—The Scharrer and Betz homes at the home-stead site are burned, either intentionally or by careless campers. The beach cabins are burned by accident or arson.

1956—Clinton Washburn sells Honeymoon Island to Arthur Vining Davis; interest in developing the island property is rekindled. Honeymoon Island property changes hands several times over the coming years.

1959—The Dunedin City Commission makes an agreement with the owners

Myrtle with granddaughter Terry.

of Honeymoon Island, Curlew Properties, Inc. (CPI), to seek dredge and fill rights for a vast area surrounding Honeymoon Island and to convey these rights to Curlew Properties, Inc. on the basis that CPI will in turn do two things for the city: 1) Create a free causeway to Honeymoon Island, and 2) Create a 300 ft. x 2,500 ft. public beach. According to records from that time (detailed in a "Preliminary Generalized Use Plan") CPI's intention is to increase the size of the island by 3,000 acres and to pursue intense development of the island. A road would run south to Caladesi, Hurricane Pass would be filled. The plans show the Dunedin City parcel and homestead parcel will be a public park, with fingers of residential land to be dredged and filled to the east side of Caladesi. No one could yet imagine the public outcry in defense of Caladesi and Honeymoon Island.

1964—The three-mile Dunedin Causeway to Honeymoon Island is completed. The building up of the causeway acts as a dike, impeding the flow of tidal water in St. Joseph Sound, and the dredging work once again impacts the sea grass ecosystem. As the causeway is completed, construction begins on condominiums that stand today east of the entrance to Honeymoon Island State Park. This is the initial phase of the planned residential development. Curlew Properties Inc. experiences financial difficulties and the company is reorganized as Honeymoon Island Development Corporation (HIDC).

The Dunedin Causeway under construction.

1964-1965—Gerald (Jerry) Rehm is appointed to the Dunedin City Commission. With personal passion, consummate diplomacy and dogged determination he organizes an effective civic campaign that results in Caladesi Island making it onto the list of park sites to be recommended to the State Cabinet. • The idea of preserving Caladesi as a state park for public use, and of NOT developing it commercially, was "equated to building a stairway to the moon. Sure, it was a good idea, but nothing would ever come of it." (*Dunedin Times,* Joe Castello, September 2, 1965) Due to Gerald Rehm's vital leadership and hard work, and the involvement of many citizens, the "good idea" gains credibility.

1966—Gerald Rehm, now the elected Mayor of Dunedin, asks state senator Bill Young for help, as "it was unheard of here to preserve a piece of land rather than developing it." Bill Young gets Governor Claude Kirk to take a flight over the island in a helicopter, Mayor Rehm makes the case and the Governor is interested in supporting the idea. Mayor Rehm is asked by the State to explore and establish the land value on Caladesi. There are twenty-one individual owners of the properties on Caladesi so the ensuing negotiation process, diplomatically handled by Mayor Rehm, becomes quite complex. The owners of the largest acreage lots pledge their approval of the project. The City of Dunedin Commission votes to donate the city tract to the state in an effort to sweeten the deal. This is the 84 acres that had been purchased from the state in 1937.

circa 1966—Another program of ditch digging, this time by bulldozer, directed by the mosquito control board, takes place on Caladesi and results in significant alteration to the terrain. Well-intentioned, but ill-advised, according to Myrtle; more of the mangroves and mounds are destroyed. The idea was to channel water out of the area to quell the breeding of salt marsh mosquitoes. • Today the park kayak trails at Caladesi run through some of these ditches.

1967-September 25—Governor Claude Kirk writes a personal letter to Honorable Gerald Rehm, Mayor of Dunedin. This letter rightfully states: "Now that the acquisition of Caladesi Island for a state park is a virtual reality, I want to take this opportunity to thank you, both personally and on behalf of the State of Florida, for the vital part you played in bringing about this signal accomplishment. Without your direct assistance in every phase of the lengthy and difficult negotiations, it is unlikely that we would be much closer to success today than we were at the outset two long years ago." The people of Florida are forever indebted to Gerald Rehm for his selfless contribution of time, energy and talent in the interest of preserving Caladesi as a recreational area and for a wildlife refuge.

1967—The State of Florida purchases all 653 upland acres of Caladesi Island for 2.95 million dollars. On November 1, 1967, Caladesi becomes an "official"

State park when Captain S.B. Wilson is assigned as the first superintendent. The first park office is in downtown Dunedin and one of the immediate and necessary purchases made for the new park is a boat and motor so that park personnel can get to the island and back. • In 1981 Myrtle is asked what she thinks of her previous home becoming part of a state park. She replies, "I couldn't be more pleased. That was the dream of my father, to have that preserved as a park, and I feel that is like a prayer being answered."

1967-1971—Myrtle serves as a member of the Caladesi Island State Park Advisory Council to the Florida Board of Parks.

1967-December—The unveiling of a painting, "The Scharrer Homestead on Caladesi Island" by artist Helen Pierson, is a highlight of the annual meeting of Caladesi National Bank at their Dunedin Causeway location. This painting is now part of the permanent collection of the Dunedin Historical Museum, 349 Main Street.

1968—A 60-foot fire tower, a park feature suggested by Myrtle, is installed as an attraction at Caladesi and affords a wonderful place for making lofty observations. • In 1982 it has to be removed due to safety issues, as the salt air has caused corrosion of the metal struts and bolts.

1969-1970—Herman becomes bedridden due to illness. Myrtle is very much occupied in caring for him at home. Myrtle takes driving instruction and gets her first license.

1969—Honeymoon Island Development Corp. (HIDC) is pressured by the Dunedin City Commission to make good on their promise to complete work on the public beach. The ensuing dredging operation meets with difficulty as rock, instead of sand, is encountered. As a result, what had been a crystal white sand beach is "augmented" with piles of agatized coral and limestone rocks. Rock collectors are delighted. HIDC attempts to remedy the situation by crushing the rocks and hauling sand to put back on the beach. A storm with a high tide washes the sand away, leaving the rocks exposed again. The dredge and fill permit for HIDC is allowed to lapse.

1969-1974—The Dunedin City Commission is called upon to negotiate a compromise, as the 1959 contract with CPI had allowed development of Honeymoon Island. In the years since the initial contract, philosophical changes at the public and governmental levels lead to an environmental awareness that instead favors public ownership of the barrier island property.

Further plans for commercial and residential development of Honeymoon Island meet with much opposition from local residents. The ensuing legal battle is protracted and sometimes bitter.

1970-February—SAVE (Suncoast Active Volunteers for Ecology), a grass roots citizens action group, organizes and leads a coalition (including Audubon, League of Women Voters, Conservation 70's and homeowner and boating interest groups) to protest the proposed dredge and fill permit to quadruple the size of Honeymoon Island. Scientists from local universities and colleges, the press, and several politicians join the effort and lobby the Florida Senate, Florida House, the Governor and the Cabinet to come out against the project.

1970-February 22—Eddie, Marion's fourth child, is born on Grandmother Myrtle's 75th birthday.

1970-May—In regards to the proposed dredging permit for Honeymoon, over 11,000 letters of objection are sent to the Governor and Cabinet from concerned groups and citizens, from Pinellas County and around the State. To focus further attention, a weekend "Boat-A-Thon" is organized by Bill Crown III of SAVE. Many boats anchor in the waters off Honeymoon Island while people on the shore gather to protest renewal of the dredge and fill permit.

1970-June—The Army Corps of Engineers holds a public meeting in Clearwater to hear both sides of the dispute over renewal of the Honeymoon dredge and fill permit.

1970-September 1—Herman Betz dies after a prolonged illness. Homes that he built on Clearwater Beach and in Dunedin still stand. He leaves a legacy of skillfully constructed wooden boats and useful items of furniture: desks, benches, end tables, trunks, shelves.

1970-November—Army Corps of Engineers announces the denial of the dredge and fill permit for Honeymoon Island.

1972—Marion and Eddie come to live with Myrtle in Palm Harbor.

1972-1981—Myrtle does part-time work in Dunedin and in Ozona as a companion for homebound seniors. She makes a road trip to visit New Mexico with longtime friend Elaine Hinson. Myrtle remains involved

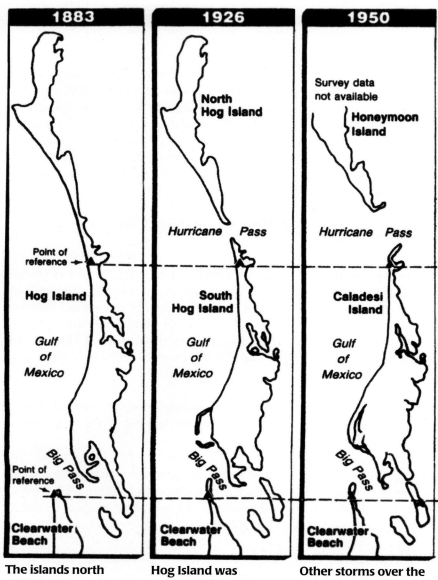

1883

1926

1950

North
Hog Island

Survey data
not available

Honeymoon
Island

Hurricane   Pass

Hurricane   Pass

Point of
reference →

Hog Island

South
Hog Island

Caladesi
Island

Gulf
of
Mexico

Gulf
of
Mexico

Gulf
of
Mexico

Big Pass

Big Pass

Big Pass

Point of
reference →

Clearwater
Beach

Clearwater
Beach

Clearwater
Beach

The islands north of Clearwater Beach known today as Caladesi and Honeymoon were one Island in 1883 and named Hog Island.

Hog Island was separated into two keys by the rushing waters of the storm of 1921, creating Hurricane Pass.

Other storms over the years helped widen Hurricane Pass, but few changes occurred through 1950 when the Dunedin Causeway was started.

The development of Hurricane Pass, 1883-1986.

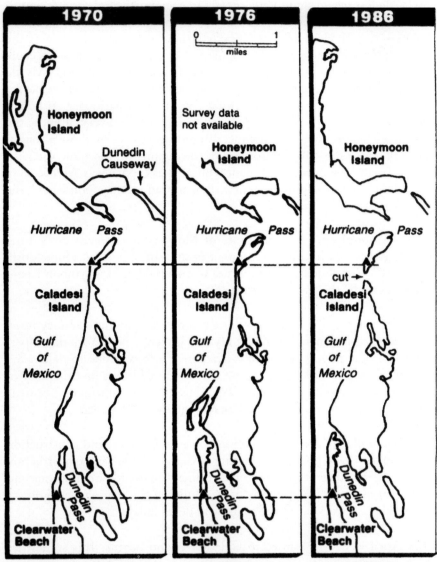

1970

1976

1986

Honeymoon Island

Dunedin Causeway

Hurricane Pass

Caladesi Island

Gulf of Mexico

Dunedin Pass

Clearwater Beach

0 miles 1

Survey data not available

Honeymoon Island

Hurricane Pass

Caladesi Island

Gulf of Mexico

Dunedin Pass

Clearwater Beach

Honeymoon Island

Hurricane Pass

cut →

Caladesi Island

Gulf of Mexico

Dunedin Pass

Clearwater Beach

By 1970, the causeway's affect on tidal flow narrowed Hurricane Pass and filled much of Dunedin Pass, formerly called Big Pass.

By 1976, Clearwater Beach had moved northward into Dunedin Pass, almost joining the southern end of Caladesi Island.

In 1985 the wind and tides of Hurricane Elena severed the north tip of Caladesi from the main island, creating a new cut into the Gulf.

Reproduced courtesy of the *St. Petersburg Times*.

with Caladesi Island State Park, mostly in a supportive role as a friend to the park personnel, especially Capt. Wilson and his wife Mary, and Cathy Wabbersen, park clerk and secretary. Myrtle is always appreciative of the efforts of the park rangers and recognizes that they do a public service, often under difficult conditions. She delivers homemade bread and "Myrtle Betz" coffee cake to the park staff, and each Christmas makes fruitcake for gift giving, a recipe from her ranching days in New Mexico. • Although frequently invited, Myrtle does not visit Caladesi Island very often, as the inevitable changes there are disconcerting to her, especially those wrought by the policy of prescribed burns and by the digging of "mosquito ditches." She prefers to remember her Caladesi home it as it once was. Myrtle stays fairly aloof from the controversies swirling around Honeymoon Island; she is in favor of its becoming a park.

1973—An application to the State of Florida Department of Natural Resources and to the Florida Cabinet is submitted by Dee Dubendorff, former SAVE president. This application requests that Honeymoon Island be purchased by the state for a park.

1974-February—The State of Florida agrees to purchase Honeymoon Island from the owners (primarily Hyman Green, a New York developer) as a future state park. The purchase agreement brings an end to stalemated litigation brought by HIDC against the State of Florida and the City of Dunedin regarding the lapse of the 1959 development agreement. Approximately 25.5 million dollars is paid incrementally over six years..

1976-September—The ranger station opens on Caladesi and construction begins on the island marina. According to Cathy Wabbersen, "Construction was a challenge, everything was made difficult by weather conditions and the need to bring all supplies by barge. Building the marina was quite an undertaking. A workday at the island was never dull."

1978-April—A ferry service to Caladesi Island begins. This somewhat isolated state park is thus accessible to the general public. The marina constructed at the island accommodates boaters and the ferry dock.

1980-1991—Myrtle continues to keep a daily diary from her home at Sutherland Bayou. She maintains written correspondence with a multitude of friends and regularly prepares meals for her invited guests. She is celebrated as a local living legend. Having rowed her boat to attend school is what really impresses the crowds. Myrtle replies, "I've always been overrated,"

Myrtle in later years with her grandchildren: Eddie (left) and Suzanne and Terry (right).

and remarks that some children walked three miles to get to school, and to her this seems more difficult.

1981-1982—Myrtle writes *Pets through the Years* (1981) and *Yesteryear I Lived In Paradise*. She writes by hand into one bound and then one loose-leaf notebook, with virtually no rewriting or revision. She completes her book in her 87th year. • Anyone who views Myrtle's original handwritten manuscript is deeply impressed with her total grasp of her subject and her succinct, focused style. Myrtle's writing reflects the way she communicated; when she had something to say it was well worth paying close attention.

1982-April 23—Honeymoon Island State Park is opened officially to the public.

1984-1985-Friends of Myrtle Betz arrange to have *Yesteryear I Lived In Paradise* printed as a surprise gift for Myrtle's 90th birthday. Myrtle has many lifelong friends and admirers who pay her the lovely tribute of assisting with this endeavor.

1985-May 18—Myrtle serves as guest of honor at a celebration event on Caladesi Island of the 50th anniversary of the founding of Florida's state park system. Marjorie Woodhouse, a friend and neighbor, takes a photo that day and afterwards paints a miniature portrait of Myrtle called "Lady from Caladesi." This painting is in a private collection.

1985—On Labor Day weekend Hurricane Elena effectively closes Dunedin Pass (once known as Big Pass) and creates two new cuts into the Gulf at the northern tip of Caladesi. In the years following, Dunedin Pass totally fills with sand and Caladesi and Clearwater Island are joined. One of the cuts at the north end is gradually filled in, also.

1989-Professor Stephen Leatherman starts his annual list of finest beaches. Caladesi consistently ranks in his top ten of America's Best Beaches.

1990-1992—Grandson Eddie is a companion to Myrtle, enabling her to remain in her own home, as is her wish. She is sought after for interviews and makes public appearances on behalf of her book. Her memory and wit remain sharply intact.

1991—A second edition of *Yesteryear*, sponsored by the Palm Harbor Junior Women's Club, is printed and sold to benefit the Henry Scharrer Memorial Scholarship Fund. In partnership with the Doorways Program, sales eventually result in the awarding of nine pre-paid college scholarships to local young people.

1992-January 2-3:30 a.m.—Myrtle Scharrer Betz dies at the age of 96. It had been Myrtle's request that her ashes be scattered in the Gulf waters. This wish is fulfilled by her great-grandson, Aaron Scharrer Fortner, with assistance from Carl Calhoun, long-time ranger at Caladesi Island State Park.

2000—Myrtle Scharrer Betz posthumously receives the honor of being declared a Great Floridian. A plaque in her honor is placed at the Dunedin Fish Market, 51 Main Street. From this location one may look out across St. Joseph Sound to Caladesi Island where, off the shoreline of Florida's most densely populated county, a sacred darkness and quiet enfold Caladesi each night.

ACKNOWLEDGEMENTS

The initial 1985 publication of *Yesteryear I Lived In Paradise* was made possible by the interest and generosity of the following friends of Myrtle Betz:

Winnie and Bouton McDougal, Chet and Ginnie Moore, Margaret and Gavin Douglas, Vivien and Robert Grant, Larry H. Dimmitt, Jr., Walter Winchester, Dorothy and Kenneth Hamlin, Helen Lindner, Naomi and David Perkins, Hazel and William E. Crown, Angela and Ben Skinner, Frances Richards Breeden, Dottie and Wallis Skinner, Gladys and Stanley Douglas, Shirley and F. L. "Gus" Cooper, Sarah and Lawrence Douglas, Carol and Joseph Alexander, Michael Sanders, Doris and Tommy Scanlan, Marian and Douglas Davis, Jessie Mae and Frank J. Betz, Bertha Springer McLean, Marjorie and Woody Woodhouse, Claire and Alan Houghton, Betty and Yancey W. Land, Frances James, Jane and Richard Kamensky, Florence Miller, Maxine Nicholson, Starr Nicholson Porter, Peg and Rodger Havens, Joree and Homer Dudley, Dorothy Douglas, Marjorie Douglas, Marge Armston, Hazel Moore Boekel, Peggy and Robert Frederiksen, Mary and Donald Fortner, Dorothy M. Marsh, Claudia Mitchell, Shirley and Wilmer James, Charlotte and Elmer Quick, Mary and Albert Springer, Thelma Bolger, Judith L. Stokes, W. Kelly Prior, Walter K. Prior, Jeannette and Waldense Malouf, Louise and George Saunders, Jeannette Saunders Flynn, Marilynn and Robert Edmunds, Ruth and Buford Webb, Sadie and Cecil Englebert, Zara and Joseph Mobley, Patricia and Russell Fought, "Cappy" Jessie Landa, Jane and John Tischner, Stanley M. Miller, Helen Pierson (cover design), Cathy Wabbersen, Cathy Shaw, Michelle and John Homer, Terry and Robert Fortner, Suzanne M. Thorp, Gerald M. Thorp, Louise Bolger Riddle, Edith Grant, Alfred Grant.

The 1991 edition, published by Palm Harbor Chronicle Publishing Project, was sponsored by the Palm Harbor Junior Women's Club under the leadership of Susan Latvala. Financial support was also provided by the Pinellas County Historical Society and by Sun Bank–Palm Lake Office, Republic Bank–Palm Harbor Office, and Gulf Bank of Dunedin. The 1991 revised edition was edited by Sharon Kirby, Terrance M. and Marjorie E. Fox, of Direct Response Marketing, with cover design by Sue Ellen Adams. The proceeds for the 1991 edition, above the cost of publication, went to the Henry Scharrer Memorial Scholarship Fund. It had been Myrtle's expressed wish to help one young person to experience a college education via a scholarship given in memory of her father. In fact, as the 5,000 second edition books sold, nine prepaid college scholarships were awarded in partnership with the Doorways Program of Pinellas County.

As copies of the previous editions became scarce, many requests to reprint a revised edition were made. In our effort to prepare this 2007 edition, we first want to gratefully acknowledge the invaluable assistance of our immediate family members: Marion Ann Thorp, Rev. Robert N. Fortner, Jennifer R. Fortner, and Aaron Scharrer Fortner. We extend our appreciation also to our brothers, David Scharrer Thorp and Eddie Davis Thorp, who each express talents and wisdom influenced by Myrtle.

We wish to especially acknowledge our heartfelt gratitude to our brilliant and admirable aunt, Alice Thorp Duxbury, who cheerfully and generously gave hours and days of her time to prepare the manuscript for publishing, and who wrote and spoke encouraging words to us throughout the entire process.

We are thankful for the expertise and knowledgeable, dedicated work of all those associated with the University of Tampa Press, especially Dr. Richard Mathews, Sean Donnelly, Chris Janus, and Angela Terry.

For assistance with the maps, illustrations, and photos we are grateful to Lisa Young; Linda Cron; Barbara J. Carrier; Marcia M. Colby, GIS applications specialist with the Pinellas County Environmental Lands Division; Earl (Gene) Quinn, senior environmental specialist with the Clean Marina and Pollution Prevention Program of Pinellas County Environmental Management; Sally Cole Braem, biological scientist, Honeymoon Island State Park; Brian K. Smith, planning director, and Susan Kinney, secretary, Pinellas County Planning Department; Rick Woodhouse, Gabriel's Inn of Pennsylvania; Vincent Luisi, executive director, and Sandy Kinzer, administrative assistant, of the Dunedin Historical Society Museum, Inc.; Kathy Hughes, photo reprint coordinator with the *St. Petersburg Times*; Heather Bonds of CopyPros of Palm Harbor; N. Adam Watson of the State Archives of Florida; and Jim and James Ronayne of FASTFRAME Expert Picture Framing. To Richard W. Estabrook, director of the West Central Region, Florida Archaeology Network, we owe a very particular thank-you for helping resolve an issue having to do with the site map of Caladesi. Thank you to the staff of the University of South Florida, Tampa, Special Collections Library, especially Keli Rylance, Paul E. Camp, and Richard Bernardi.

We want to thank J. B. Dobkin, volunteer archivist for Heritage Village at Pinewood Cultural Park in Pinellas County, who initially recommended this book to the University of Tampa Press, and the staff of Heritage Village—Ellen Babb, historian; Alison Giesen, curator of collections; Lanie Hamel, archivist-registrar; and Jan Luth, director.

[187]

Thank you to Gary Mormino, professor of history at the University of South Florida, St. Petersburg, and to Lynne Mormino, for their interest and encouragement.

We are indebted to those who have contributed their expertise to aspects of the manuscript. Betty Wargo, Dr. Walter K. "Sweet-Pea" Taylor, and Carmel van Hoek gave special attention to plant and animal species references. Paul Trunk, with the Clearwater Audubon Society, looked over Myrtle's bird list and gave counsel. Sharon Kirby Lamm, a neighbor and personal friend of Myrtle, contributed to all three editions of *Yesteryear*. Susan Putnam-Vuellers assisted Suzanne in edits to this edition.

Special thanks to those who helped scrutinize, corroborate, and clarify the Timeline portion: Kelly Victory, biologist and environmental educator; Christopher Still, native Floridian and outstanding fine artist; Tommy Walsh, meteorologist; Peter Krulder, park manager, Honeymoon Island State Park; Bill Gruber, assistant park manager, and Carl Calhoun, Park Ranger, Caladesi Island State Park; Cathy Harlan Shaw, administrative assistant, Honeymoon Island Administration; Vincent Luisi, executive director of the Dunedin Historical Society Museum; and Dr. Maxine Jones, Professor of History at Florida State University. Much appreciation is extended to Mike Sanders, Bill Wallace, and Bob Delack of the Clearwater Historical Society for their encouragement and active, knowledgeable assistance. Invaluable input for the Timeline was received from those who personally knew Myrtle and/or who participated in the events as detailed. Thanks everlasting to Gerald S. (Jerry) Rehm, the individual most essential to Caladesi Island becoming a state park. Thank you to Vivien Skinner Grant, who has participated fully in endeavors to promote the finest remembrances of Dunedin's past history and who has the family connections and historical knowledge to make her Dunedin's "first lady." Thank you to Woody Register who has an amazing memory and a wealth of stories to tell embracing all aspects of life in Pinellas County, and who has taken an active role throughout his nine decades of living here. Thanks to Cathy Wabbersen, who served as Secretary Specialist for Caladesi Island State Park, 1975-1994. A debt of gratitude is owed to the many citizen activists who worked tirelessly in the effort to have Honeymoon Island declared as a state park. Thank you to Dee Dubendorff for assistnace in detailing those efforts. Thank you to Verna Daniel (Blackburn), Jim Jenkins, Charley and Winona Jones, active and knowledgeable people who provided personal remembrances that helped with details of the Timeline, and to journalist and local historian Leland M. Hawes Jr., who read the final draft.

Through three years of effort a multitude of people have shared a kind word of encouragement, provided technical assistance, or verified an essential bit of information. Please know that your help was appreciated, and we want to thank you, even if we are unable to place your name in this acknowledgement.

It is our sincere wish that in *Yesteryear I Lived in Paradise* the reader will be inspired by Myrtle's quiet accomplishments, her dedicated devotion to family, her deep appreciation for her Florida birthplace. It seems these were the gifts given by her father and mother, and we would wish every person in our world could have such a sense of belonging to the place where they are born. Thank you to the many people who have kept Myrtle and Henry Scharrer's memory alive through their interest and to all those who have clamored for *Yesteryear* in this third edition.

Gratitude is extended to those who gave pre-purchase orders and supported this edition going to press: Sandpearl Resort on Clearwater Beach (JMC Design and Development, Inc.), Friends of the Island Parks, Florida Beach Services (especially Shane Bittaker), Linda Taylor of It's Our Nature, Inc.

To Christopher Still, whose oil painting graces the cover, and to his wife, Kelly Victory, an extra thank-you must be given. During the many months of working on details for this edition they provided pep talks, inspiration, and new contacts with knowledgeable people. This edition would not have happened in the present form without their energetic participation. As serendipitous circumstance would have it, the work that we were doing to bring *Yesteryear* to press happened during the same years that Christopher has been immersed in painting two large works for installation at the Sandpearl Resort being built on Clearwater Island. Christopher's paintings have evolved to incorporate images from the rich historical and environmental features of both Caladesi and Clearwater Islands. It was a great blessing that the research in which Christopher was deeply involved was so complementary to the work that we were doing to get *Yesteryear* ready.

Heartfelt thanks to the dedicated managers, rangers, staff, and volunteers of Caladesi and Honeymoon Island State Parks, who have served the public as they protect what can be saved of the habitat and history of these barrier islands. In honor of these dedicated men and women of the past and present, a portion of the proceeds of this edition will be dedicated to the Henry Scharrer Memorial Fund, a not-for-profit organization. Funds will underwrite specific projects at Caladesi and Honeymoon Island State Parks. *−T. F. & S. T.*

ABOUT THE BOOK

The text of this book is set in Adobe Caslon Pro, adapted from the famous English fonts of William Caslon first cast in the 1720s. The digital rendering preserves many of Caslon's original features, including its graceful "st" and "ct" ligatures.

Caslon used seventeenth century Dutch types as his models, but he added notable refinements. As the American printer Daniel Berkeley Updike explains in *Printing Types*: "He introduced into his fonts a quality of interest, a variety of design, and a delicacy of modelling which few Dutch types possessed. Dutch fonts were monotonous, but Caslon's fonts were not so. . . . Their secret—a perfection of the whole derived from harmonious but not necessarily perfect individual letterforms." Caslon's types became immensely popular in Colonial America. The first printings of the Declaration of Independence and the Constitution were set in Caslon, and it was the typeface of choice for Benjamin Franklin. It continued to be widely used by American printers throughout the nineteenth and early twentieth centuries.

The script font used for titling within the book is P22 Cezanne, adapted from the handwriting of the famous French artist Paul Cezanne by the P22 Type Foundry of Buffalo, New York. The book was designed and typeset by Sean Donnelly, Richard Mathews, and Ana Montalvo at the University of Tampa Press. It was printed on acid-free Huron Gloss Enamel recycled text paper in support of the Green Press Initiative by Thomson-Shore of Dexter, Michigan.